Story of th

Frank Moss

Alpha Editions

This edition published in 2024

ISBN : 9789362997807

Design and Setting By
Alpha Editions
www.alphaedis.com
Email - info@alphaedis.com

As per information held with us this book is in Public Domain.
This book is a reproduction of an important historical work. Alpha Editions uses the best technology to reproduce historical work in the same manner it was first published to preserve its original nature. Any marks or number seen are left intentionally to preserve its true form.

PERSECUTION OF NEGROES

BY

Roughs and Policemen, in the City
of New York, August, 1900.

STATEMENT AND PROOFS WRITTEN AND COM-
PILED BY FRANK MOSS AND ISSUED BY THE
CITIZENS' PROTECTIVE LEAGUE.

STATEMENT OF THE PERSECUTION.

The riots and persecutions described in this pamphlet occurred mainly in the 20th Police Precinct, which is under the command of Acting Captain John Cooney, and within the jurisdiction of Inspector Walter L. Thompson. Chief William S. Devery resides in the precinct, near the scene of the disorder.

The district has a large colored population, and mixed with it are many dissolute and lawless white persons.

On August the 12th last a Negro named Arthur Harris was with his wife at 41st Street and 8th Avenue. He says that he left her to buy a cigar, and when he returned he found her in the grasp of a man in citizen's dress. This man was a police officer, named Robert J. Thorpe, who had arrested her, as he claimed, for "soliciting." Harris says that he did not know Thorpe was an officer, and that he attempted to rescue his wife. The policeman struck Harris with his club, and Harris retaliated with his penknife, inflicting a mortal wound, and then ran away.

Thorpe was attached to the 20th Precinct, and was much liked by his comrades. Policemen thronged his home, and his funeral, on August 16th, was attended by Chief Devery, Inspector Thompson, and other officials.

Harris, the murderer, had disappeared, and many policemen who were interested in Thorpe were seized with a desire of vengeance on Negroes generally. During the day of the funeral there were rumors of coming trouble, and those colored people who have illicit dealings with the police—keepers of gambling, disorderly, and badger houses—seeing the signs of coming trouble, closed their places and kept off the streets. Several officers told informants of mine that they were going to punish the Negroes that night. There are numerous gangs of rowdies in the district who are hostile to Negroes and friendly with the unofficial powers that are now potent in police affairs. There was an understanding between the forces that night that resulted in the holding of the streets for hours by crowds of roughs who raced up and down Broadway, 7th and 8th Avenues, and the side streets from 34th to 42nd Streets in pursuit of Negroes, and were not attacked by the police except in one or two cases where they invaded Broadway hotels hunting for colored men.

The unanimous testimony of the newspaper reports was that the mobs could have been broken and destroyed immediately and with little difficulty. In many instances of brutality by the mob policemen stood by and made no effort to protect the Negroes who were assailed. They ran with the crowds in pursuit of their prey; they took defenseless men who ran to them for protection and threw them to the rioters, and in many cases they beat and clubbed men and women more brutally than the mob did. They were absolutely unrestrained by their superior officers. It was the night sticks of the police that sent a stream of bleeding colored men to the hospital, and that made the station house in West 37th Street look like a field hospital in the midst of battle. Men who were taken to the station house by officers and men in the station house were beaten by policemen without mercy, and their cries of distress made sleep impossible for those who lived in the rear of the station house.

Colored men being denied official protection, many of them obtained weapons, and if they were found armed, or if revolvers were found in their houses, then official brutality was redoubled.

The tumult of August 15th was repeated on a smaller scale on the night of the 16th, but public attention had been directed to the shameful conduct of our "guardians of the peace," and the precinct swarmed with reporters and sightseers. Then the dilatory officials speedily quelled the riot and ended the punishment of the Negroes.

In the courts many false charges were made by policemen; and although some Negroes were discharged by the magistrates, others were convicted and punished on the false testimony of their accusers. One magistrate commented severely on the comparatively small number of white men that were arraigned before him for rioting.

Had a force of regular soldiers been sent to quell such a disturbance, and had it failed so utterly and so long as did the police, and had the soldiers abandoned their duty, and vied with the roughs in beating the men whom they should have protected, undoubtedly some guilty privates would have been punished—but the severest penalty would have fallen on their incompetent or derelict commanders. The commanders in this case were Acting Captain Cooney, Inspector Thompson, and Chief Devery.

The newspapers told of the shocking outrage, and printed many specific cases of cruelty, giving the addresses of the victims and the circumstances of their persecution. By this and other means the Police Commissioners and the Mayor were fully apprised of the facts. There was no suspicion of politics in the universal demand that went up for a prompt and efficient investigation and for the severe punishment of the offenders. This request was unheeded, until the acting Mayor called on the Police Commissioners to investigate the conduct of their subordinates. The Commissioners delayed, knowing full well how such cases deteriorate by delay, and after several weeks announced that they would investigate.

The colored people of the city, realizing their unexpected danger as a race, and discovering the surprising unwillingness of the city authorities to punish their assailants and to protect them in the future, formed "The Citizens' Protective League." This society and the Society for the Prevention of Crime and the City Vigilance League communicated with the Mayor in writing and urged him to hold an investigation or to direct the Commissioner of Accounts to hold one for him. His answer was that the whole matter was in the hands of the Board of Police. A number of Negroes who had been injured retained Israel Ludlow, Esq., to bring suits against the city for damages inflicted on them by the mob. He filed with the Police Commissioners the affidavit of William J. Elliott, who had been clubbed in the station house. The Police Board began its "investigation" by calling Elliott and his witnesses on the 7th of September. The examination of witnesses was conducted by the President of the Board, Bernard J. York, and, with the approval of the Board, he refused to give subpœnas to Mr. Ludlow, and refused to allow him or any other lawyer to examine or cross-examine any witnesses, or to suggest any step to be taken. Elliott and all other colored witnesses were examined by the President as hostile parties, and their testimony was controverted by the policemen who were called at once and were carefully nursed and led by him. Glaring discrepancies and disagreements in their testimony were passed over in spite of specific protests by Mr. Ludlow. The writer appeared on behalf of the societies that had memorialized the Mayor, and filed a complaint of inefficiency and neglect of duty against the Captain, the Inspector, and the Chief of Police, and announced that he had much testimony to offer on the specifications, but insisted on his right to examine his own witnesses and to cross-examine the police witnesses. These rights were emphatically denied, and the complaint was disdainfully pigeonholed.

The Protective League separately asked the Mayor for justice; he responded that the whole matter was with the Police Board, and he made the same response to Mr. Ludlow, who complained to him of the farce that was being enacted at Police Headquarters. The hearing was continued several days. Witnesses were examined superficially in eight cases of cruelty by policemen, and were controverted by double the number of policemen, and it was suddenly announced that the hearings were closed. Claims of sixteen Negroes against the city were then on file in the Comptroller's office, the names and addresses of many more victims had appeared in the newspapers, and the writer had announced that he had in his possession over forty affidavits of police brutality. The "investigation" was a palpable sham.

At this date not a single complaint has been preferred by the Chief, the Inspector, the Captain, or the Commissioners against any police officer for brutality or neglect of duty during the riots.

On September 12th a great meeting was held at Carnegie Hall to protest against the brutality and against the failure of the city authorities to act, and to take measures for the prevention of such outbreaks in the future. Fully thirty-five hundred people attended, and listened to addresses by Rev. R. S. MacArthur, D.D., Rev. D. W. Cook, D.D., Rev. C. T. Walker, D.D., Rev. W. H. Brooks, D.D., Rev. Bishop W. B. Derrick, D.D., Miss M. R. Lyons, Hon. D. M. Webster.

A subscription was started, and measures were taken to make the Citizens' Protective League a permanent and a vital institution.

The League and its representatives are using every possible lawful measure to secure justice to its people, and to vindicate their right to live in peace. They are having a difficult task to get a hearing. Several cases have been brought by it in the Magistrates' Court, but they are difficult to carry in the face of a solid and lusty swearing lot of policemen, and they cannot show the crime in its mass, and cannot reveal the responsibility of the higher officials for the outbreak and for the failure to discover and punish the guilty policemen and their commanders.

The Mayor has abundant authority to hear the matter, but he has washed his hands of it, and the Police Board has not hesitated to write another page of its damning history. There is no other way open for a full and connected presentation of the case to the public except by legal process through the Mayor and the Commissioners. A Grand Jury investigation was had, and resulted in no indictment. Such an investigation is necessarily held behind closed doors, and the sole question is whether there is sufficient evidence to warrant the indictment of a specific individual for a specific act, unrelated to other acts, and with a reasonable probability of conviction.

I have advised the Citizens' Protective League of the great barriers to be overcome in securing the conviction of even a patrolman, and of the inadequacy of a criminal proceeding in an attempted presentation of the great wrong that the Negroes have suffered. They need the sympathy and support of the good people of New York to secure a vindication, and to prevent a recurrence of the outbreak. Under my advice the appended affidavits have been secured, and are now printed, so that they may be read and considered in their relation to each other. I may say that with hardly an exception the affiants have shown themselves to be respectable, hard-working men and women. The dissolute Negroes who are so often seen lounging about the "Tenderloin" and its neighborhood are not to be found among the witnesses. They are the friends of the police, contributing very largely to their comfort and happiness, and it is quite clear that they had their warning and kept out of the way.

With this simple introduction, I present the affidavits, confident that they will speak for themselves, and that they will lead to the condemnation of the high official criminals, and contribute to the overthrow of the infernal system that they represent.

Brutality and insolence of policemen have increased greatly, and the Police Commissioners seldom, if ever, convict officers for these offenses. Humble citizens of all races to-day are in more danger from policemen's clubs than they are from the assaults of criminals. The inaction of the Commissioners in the cases of the Negroes is entirely consistent with their general conduct in all citizens' complaints.

FRANK MOSS.

Dated October 1, 1900.

City and County of New York, ss.:

P. A. Johnson, M.D., being duly sworn, deposes and says: I reside at 203 West 33rd Street, and am engaged in the active practice of my profession at that address. On Thursday morning, August 16th, 1900, about ten A. M., I heard a noise in the street, and going to the window I saw a colored man trying to get into one of the flats on the opposite side of the street. He failed, and went east to the corner saloon, kept by a man Gallagher, and entered. After he went in I noticed three policemen in the saloon. Almost immediately a mob came down 7th Avenue. At the saloon they commenced to shout, "Bring him out, we'll lynch him!" Several of the rioters went into the saloon, and in a few minutes they came out again and formed in a semicircle, evidently waiting for something. The police officers appeared with the colored man, clubbing him unmercifully. They then shoved him into the mob. He managed to get through them and ran down the street, and I heard him shortly shouting for mercy, saying, "For God's sake don't kill me, I have a wife and children." Deponent has been informed that two of the officers ran down the street after him and knocked him senseless.

P. A. JOHNSON.

Sworn to before me this 10th day of September, 1900.

GEO. P. HAMMOND, JR., Notary Public (164), N. Y. County.

City and County of New York, ss.:

Stephen Small, being duly sworn, deposes and says: I reside at the northwest corner of 7th Avenue and 34th Street. On Wednesday evening, August 15th, 1900, I went to the home of a sick brother on Lexington Avenue, and started then to go to my lodge on 29th Street near 7th Avenue, and had reached 8th Avenue and 41st Street, opposite Driggs' saloon, when two officers jumped on the car. One hit me on the head with his club, and the other struck me in the eye with his club. A white man interfered, and the police desisted. I stayed on the car, and when we had gone a little further the mob boarded it and attacked me. The car had quite a number of women in it, who began to scream, and some of them told me to get under the seat, which I did, and it proceeded down the avenue. I reached the neighborhood of Hudson Street House of Relief, where the white gentleman who interfered in the first instance took me, and where I had my head bandaged. I could not get home that evening, and I remained in a cellar in 30th Street between 6th and 7th Avenues. The next morning I started to get home, and had reached the corner of 32nd Street and 7th Avenue, when I was stopped by an officer who wanted to know where I was going, and what weapon I had on me. I told him I had nothing on me. He said, "You look as if you had been in the scrap. They ought to have killed you; get out of here." As he said this he struck me across the back with his club, and I yet am unable to lay flat on my back without suffering extreme pain. Deponent further states that he was perfectly sober and was not creating any disturbance, and that the assault by the police officers was entirely unjustified and an outrage.

his
STEPHEN x SMALL.
mark

Sworn to before me this 11th day of September, 1900.

GEO. P. HAMMOND, JR., Notary Public (164), N. Y. County.

City and County of New York, ss.:

Oscar Slaughter, being duly sworn, deposes and says: I reside at 225 West 32nd Street. On Wednesday, August 15th, 1900, I boarded an 8th Avenue car at 32nd Street, starting to go to my sister's in West 62nd Street. I had got as far as 36th Street and 8th Avenue, when a mob led by three or four police officers surrounded the car and jumped on it. The police officers immediately commenced to club me. One of the rioters shouted, "Pull him off and kill him!" The officers pulled me off of the car and commenced to club me. They hit me on the head and pulled me to the street. I was kicked and beaten while I lay there, and after the mob had gone and I recovered somewhat I dragged myself to 42nd Street and 6th Avenue, and from there I went to 32nd Street between 6th and 7th Avenues. On my way there I attempted to go down 34th Street, but a white man met me and said, "Don't go down there, you'll get killed." I then tried to go down 33rd Street, but a white gentleman advised me not to go that way, as I would be killed, and said that even if he went down there and did not join in he would be jumped on. I then went to 32nd Street, where a number of colored men had taken refuge in a hallway, and where I was advised to stay all night. I stayed there a while and then took a chance in getting to my home down the block, which I succeeded in doing. Deponent is informed that an officer went into the aforesaid hallway after deponent had left, and clubbed and beat a man who lived in the house, and took him to the station house. Deponent declares that he was perfectly sober, and was creating no disturbance whatever, and that the said assault was entirely unjustified and an outrage.

OSCAR SLAUGHTER.

Sworn to before me this 11th day of September, 1900.

GEO. P. HAMMOND, JR., Notary Public (164), N. Y. County.

State of New York, City and County of New York, ss.:

Joseph Frasier, being duly sworn, deposes and says: I live at 331 West 37th Street, New York City. On August 15th, at quarter past eleven in the night, I was on my way to work on an 8th Avenue car going downtown. A crowd rushed towards the car and yelled, "Lynch the nigger!" A policeman who jumped on the car hit me on the head with his club and knocked out a tooth and beat me on the arms, back, and body until I was nearly senseless. The policeman asked me whether I wanted to go to the station or to the hospital. I said I wanted to go to my work, though the blood was running over my face so that I could hardly see. A passenger helped me until I recovered slightly, and helped me on another car and into a drug store, where I received aid. The street was filled with a rough crowd, patrol wagon, and ambulance. The people cried out from the windows, protesting against the beating, and called out "Shame!" I was laid up for weeks, and am hardly able to walk now, as I am still lame and sore. I work for Davenport, 94 Park Place, and it was my duty to get to the stable about eleven o'clock to go to New Jersey for produce.

JOSEPH FRASIER.

Sworn to before me this 11th day of September, 1900.

STEPHEN B. BRAGUE, Notary Public (125), N. Y. County.

City and County of New York, ss.:

Adolphus Cooks, being duly sworn, deposes and says: I reside at No. 243 West 32nd Street, and work for the Anchor Steamship Company, foot of West 24th Street, as a longshoreman. On Tuesday morning, August 14th, 1900, I went to work for the said company, worked all that day, all that night, and until Wednesday night at 10:30 P. M.—39½ consecutive hours. At the said hour I left the pier at the foot of West 24th Street, and walked east on 24th Street, and when I reached the northwest corner of 8th Avenue and 24th Street a white gentleman advised me not to go up 8th Avenue, as there was a riot up there and they were fighting "like he did not know what." I continued east on 24th Street until I reached the northwest corner of 7th Avenue and 24th Street, when I met another white man who advised me not to go up 7th Avenue, as there was a riot in progress, and that they were fighting at that time in the neighborhood of 41st Street and 37th Street, but, thinking that I could get home in 32nd Street before the riot could get down to that street, I started uptown on the west side of 7th Avenue, and had reached the northwest corner of 7th Avenue and 28th Street, when I saw three officers coming down 7th Avenue. In the meantime three other colored men, whom I did not know, had caught up with me, and were walking behind me. I had gone about one hundred feet north of the aforesaid corner when I saw the three officers break into a run in our direction. I was grabbed by one of them, while the other two chased the three men who had come behind us and overtook them and clubbed them; the officer who had me immediately, without saying a word, struck me on the body with his club; then between the blows he said, "Get out of here, you black son of a b———!" One of the blows he aimed at my head, but I threw up my arm and received the blow on it. It was such a severe blow that I was lame in it for quite some days. I escaped from him as soon as I could, and ran to 28th Street, and down 28th Street to No. 211. I ran into the hallway and out into the back yard, where I stayed all night in fear of my life. The officer followed me, and when I ran into the hallway he clubbed the colored people who were on the front stoop, and drove them into the house. During the heavy rainstorm Wednesday night and early

Thursday morning I took refuge in a small place that led into the cellar of the said house. Thursday morning about six o'clock I ventured out and went towards the dock at the foot of West 24th Street, where I intended to go to work again, and had reached 8th Avenue between 25th and 26th Streets, when I saw two police officers on the opposite side of the street, one of whom started to run towards me, but his companion stopped him, and drew him back. Deponent states further that if he had not been interfered with and clubbed by the police officer he could have reached his home in safety, and that he saw no signs of a disturbance, such as a large crowd of people, as far as he could see up the avenue; that deponent was watching for such signs by reason of his having been warned twice. Deponent also declares that he can identify the officer who clubbed him; that he knows him by sight, and that, about a month before the said clubbing, the same officer had come to him at his home, where he lived at that time, in West 28th Street, and had told him that the roundsman had got him, and that he had given him as an excuse that he was at the house where deponent then lived and was quelling a disturbance there, and asked deponent to verify that statement if the roundsman asked him. Deponent promised so to do, notwithstanding the fact that nothing of the kind had occurred there, and promised to do so simply to get the officer out of trouble. That the officer's first name is "Joe," and that he is attached to the 20th Precinct. Deponent further declares that he was perfectly sober, and that the assault by the officer was unwarranted and an outrage upon a peaceable citizen.

his
ADOLPHUS x COOKS.
mark

Sworn to before me this 4th day of September, 1900.

GEO. P. HAMMOND, JR., Notary Public (164), N. Y. County.

City and County of New York, ss.:

Eugene Porter, being duly sworn, deposes and says: I reside at 202 West 49th Street. On Wednesday, August 15th, 1900, between the hours of nine and ten P. M., I was walking uptown on the west side of 7th Avenue, on my way home. Everything about the neighborhood was quiet. There were no signs of a disturbance, and I had not heard of any trouble between the colored people and the white folks. I had reached a point about one hundred feet north of 37th Street on 7th Avenue, when I met a group of policemen, about six or eight in number. One of them said to me, "What are you doing here, you black son of a b——?" and without waiting for an answer struck me over the head with his club, felling me to the sidewalk, and continued to strike me about the body. I struggled to my feet, and implored the officers to spare my life, but they continued to club me and left me unconscious on the sidewalk. When I came to I arose to my feet and crawled home. After I reached home I got my young son to accompany me to the New York Hospital, where my wounds were dressed by Dr. Kenyon, of the Hospital Staff, who put fourteen stitches in my head. Deponent states further that he is troubled to this day with his head, as a result of the injuries received at the hands of the police, and he fears that it may yet seriously interfere with his following his business. Deponent states further that he is engaged in the business of horse and dog clipping, and that he can refer to the following-named persons for whom he has done work at various times: E. S. Odell, proprietor of the Saratoga Stables, 690 Madison Avenue, who has known him from infancy. Dr. H. D. Gill, Veterinary Surgeon, 57th Street and 2nd Avenue. G. W. Lynch, Morton Boarding Stables, Morton and Washington Streets. Joseph Hartshorn, 168 East 68th Street.

EUGENE PORTER.

Sworn to before me this 4th day of September, 1900.

GEO. P. HAMMOND, JR., Notary Public (164), N. Y. County.

City and County of New York, ss.:

Richard C. Creech, being duly sworn, deposes and says that he resides at No. 137 West 53rd Street. That on Wednesday morning, August 15th, 1900, he had been to visit a friend at No. 312 West 45th Street, and left there at about 10:45 P. M. and walked to 8th Avenue, and had reached the corner of 8th Avenue and 45th Street, when he was set upon by a gang of rioters, and assaulted by them. That he shouted "Police!" and seeing two officers on the east side of the avenue, corner of 45th Street, he ran towards them when he saw them coming towards him and slackened his pace, thinking that they were coming to his assistance. When they came up to him, without saying a word, they commenced clubbing him, and knocked him unconscious on the sidewalk. He lay there unconscious for some time, he does not know exactly how long, but when he came to he found one of the policeman standing over him, and when he scrambled to his feet the policeman said, "Well, you black son of a b———, I guess you will be good now, won't you? Get out of here as quick as you can!" He then went towards Broadway, and on Broadway between 45th and 46th Streets engaged a cab to take him home, and when he arrived home found that his pocketbook, containing thirty-six dollars in money and a pawnticket for a watch, was gone. He also lost his hat and an umbrella. He sent for his physician, Dr. Robert L. Cooper, 156 West 53rd Street, who took three stitches in his scalp and dressed other wounds on his arm and hand, the result of the clubbing.

RICHARD C. CREECH.

Sworn to before me this 1st day of September, 1900.

GEO. P. HAMMOND, JR., Notary Public (164), N. Y. County.

City and County of New York, ss.:

Duncan James, of No. 238 West 40th Street, engaged in business at 84 and 86 Greene Street, care of G. Blum & Brother, being duly sworn, says: On Wednesday, August 15th, I left the store and went to my tutor at West 124th Street. I left there at ten P. M., and when I reached 43rd Street and 8th Avenue three men jumped on the car and struck me in the face. Passengers advised me not to get off at 40th Street. When I arrived at 34th Street men saw me on the car, and when it reached 33rd Street the car stopped suddenly and everybody jumped off. The car was surrounded by a mob. I had no weapon or protection but a cane. I kept them off the best I could. About twelve officers came and took me from the mob. They took me about one hundred and fifty feet from 8th Avenue in 33rd Street West, and as they turned me loose the officers pounded me severely with clubs over my head, arms, and shoulders, telling me to run. I had then lost my hat, cane, and books. I went back to my teacher's house and stayed all night. I was the only negro man there. In West 33rd Street a man gave me a hat. I could find him. I begged the officers to lock me up for protection, and they would not. Dr. Swinburne treated me.

DUNCAN JAMES.

Sworn to before me this 31st day of August, 1900.

FRANK MOSS, Notary Public, N. Y. County.

City and County of New York, ss.:

Mack Thomas, being duly sworn, deposes and says:

I reside at 238 West 40th Street. On Wednesday, August 15th, 1900, I attended the St. Paul Baptist Church in West 43rd Street, and at about ten P. M. left for home. Knowing that the rioters were at work, I decided, instead of taking my usual route home, to go to 9th Avenue and transfer to 34th Street, to 7th Avenue, and thence back to 40th Street, thinking by that means to be able to avoid the rioters and reach home in safety. I boarded a 9th Avenue car at 43rd Street and transferred at 9th Avenue, and had reached the corner of 8th Avenue and 34th Street, when I saw a mob on the corner, and heard them shout, "There's two on the car; go after them, get them; lynch the niggers!" I stayed on the car until the mob boarded the car, when I jumped off and ran east on 34th Street pursued by the mob, several members of which struck me with their fists, but with no serious result. I had got so far as the middle of the block when I met four or five officers, one of whom stepped in front of me and struck me a blow with his club on the head, cutting it open. When he did so he said, "Who hit you?" I said nothing; then he said, "Get on the car, you black son of a b——, and get home out of here!" I got on the car and reached home without any further interference. Deponent declares it to be his belief that if he had not been stopped by the police, and struck by them, he would have reached his home without any serious injury; not mentioning the fact that the police made no attempt whatever to interfere with the mob. Deponent further declares that he would prefer to have taken his chances with the mob than to have met the said police officers. Deponent further declares that he was perfectly sober, was proceeding quietly on his way home, and was taking extraordinary measures to reach his home in safety and without violence.

MACK THOMAS.

Sworn to before me this 5th day of September, 1900.

GEO. P. HAMMOND, JR., Notary Public (164), N. Y. County.

City and County of New York, ss.:

Miss Belle Johnson, being duly sworn, deposes and says:

I reside at 275 West 39th Street. On Wednesday evening, August 15th, 1900, between nine and ten o'clock, I heard a disturbance in the street, and going to my window on 8th Avenue I saw a crowd of people on the sidewalk, and saw them rush toward a Negro boy who was standing on the corner (northeast corner 39th Street and 8th Avenue) and beat him. He rushed into a delicatessen store on 8th Avenue, but was thrust out by the proprietor. When he reached the sidewalk two officers grabbed him and clubbed him and then pushed him into the crowd, saying with an oath, "Run now, for your life!" He then ran to 39th Street and east on 39th Street with fully one hundred people after him. Right after this occurrence a colored man came along, and after being attacked by the mob was knocked over towards four police officers who were standing on the corner, one of whom was Officer 6312. All four of the officers then rushed for this man and clubbed him unmercifully about the head and body. I could not stand the sight any longer and shouted to the officers that it was a shame when police officers, who were supposed to be protecting peaceable citizens, assaulted them in such a brutal manner. About this time they ceased clubbing the man and thrust him out into the crowd of rioters. This sort of thing continued during the entire night, and until the next day, as at nine A. M., when I went out on an errand, I saw a colored man, who was carrying a small sign, beaten by a crowd of roughs. I saw a number of colored persons struck who were riding on the cars, and at least six colored men clubbed by the police during this time.

BELLE JOHNSON.

Sworn to before me this 5th day of September, 1900.

Geo. P. Hammond, Jr., Notary Public (164), N. Y. County.

City and County of New York, ss.:

Mrs. Fannie Lewis, being duly sworn, deposes and says:

She has read the foregoing affidavit of Miss Belle Johnson, and that she knows of her own knowledge that the facts therein stated are true.

FANNIE LEWIS.

Sworn to before me this 5th day of September, 1900.

GEO. P. HAMMOND, JR., Notary Public (164), N. Y. County.

City and County of New York, ss.:

Chester Smith, being duly sworn, deposes and says:

I reside at No. 320 West 37th Street. I am employed in Flannery's drug store, at No. 103 West 42nd Street, and have been so employed for the last ten months. On August 15th, 1900, at about ten o'clock P. M., while going to my home, walking on the west side of 8th Avenue between 38th and 39th Streets, I saw a crowd of people, composed mostly of police officers and children. Some one in the crowd said, "There is a nigger!" pointing at me. One of the policemen ran towards me, and seeing that I was in physical danger I ran away from the place, going north to 39th Street on 8th Avenue. Somebody threw a brick at me, which struck me in the back, and then one of the policemen came up to me and struck me in the left eye with his club. My eye and my forehead are still lacerated and discolored. I then ran into the saloon at the southeast corner of 39th Street and 8th Avenue. One of the policemen ran in after me, and told me to go outside and run towards Broadway; that the mob had dispersed. I started toward the door, and as I reached it I saw that they were still waiting outside. I said to the officer as I started back into the saloon, "No, sir, I can't go out there; they'll kill me." The policeman then lifted me from the ground and threw me through the swinging door into the street. The glass in the door was broken, and I fell on my hands and knees. The policemen and the mob then began beating me, the policemen beating me with their clubs. They did not disperse the crowd or protect me from it. I then started to run towards Broadway; another policeman ran after me and struck me in the back with his club. I staggered, made one or two jumps, and fell in front of No. 236 West 39th Street. The lady of the house, a white woman, came out, and I was taken into the house by some one, I don't know whom. Two or three days after she told me that the officers soon left the house, but that the mob tried to break in, and that she told them that if they would not leave she would kill them. The lady rang for a messenger boy and sent word to my employer to call. He came and brought some bandages, etc., and bandaged my head. He then called two police officers and asked them to take me to the station house. They refused. He insisted, and they finally yielded and took me to the station house. I was treated there by a police surgeon. My employer remained with me until three o'clock the next morning. I did not work for three days after this. I saw one man treated very harshly at the station house, being clubbed by police officers, and I believe he would have been treated still worse if it had not been for the presence of reporters. I did nothing whatever to justify this brutal treatment on the part of the police officers. I believe that had it not been for the presence of my employer I would have been beaten still more. There were over twenty-five policemen in the crowd. I was unconscious part of the time. I have never been arrested in my life.

CHESTER SMITH.

Sworn to before me this 5th day of September, 1900.

GEO. P. HAMMOND, JR., Notary Public (164), N. Y. County.

On September 13th, 1900, I visited the premises No. 236 West 39th Street and found that the occupant thereof was the woman who rescued Chester Smith from the hands of the mob, and that her name is Mrs. Davenport. She stated that she did not want to make an affidavit or statement of the occurrence, but volunteered the information that she had sheltered two or three Negroes during the night of August 15th and the morning of the 16th, also that several police officers who attempted to get into her house, at the time that she rescued the said Smith, acted and spoke in an insulting manner, one of them saying, "What kind of a woman are you, to be harboring niggers?"

GEORGE P. HAMMOND, JR.

City and County of New York, ss.:

Harry L. Craig, being duly sworn, deposes and says:

I reside at No. 226 West 28th Street. I am employed as a hall boy at the apartment houses Nos. 102 and 104 East 26th Street. On August 15th, 1900, I left the apartment house a little after twelve o'clock, that being the time I usually go home. I walked on 26th Street to 6th Avenue, then turned into 6th Avenue and walked to 27th Street; I then walked on 27th Street to 8th Avenue, turned into 8th Avenue, and went into the saloon at 8th Avenue and 28th Street, southwest corner, where I had a drink, and left about 12:20, going home on 28th Street. As I neared M. Groh's Son's Brewery on that block some one hit me on the head with a club; I turned around and saw three policemen in uniform, and behind them was a mob of at least fifty men. The street was very dark. I started to run home, but one of the officers tripped me, and I fell. I was then clubbed by the police and the mob into unconsciousness. When I recovered I found that the police and the mob had left. I picked up my hat and got up, and started to walk to our house, which was only a few feet away, but I staggered and fell several times. When I reached home the lady I live with, Mrs. Wisham, washed my face with witch-hazel; my jaw was so sore that I could hardly open my mouth. For a few days after this I felt sore all over my body, from the effects of this clubbing. I was clubbed by three officers. The officers led the crowd, and did not interfere when others were beating me. They made no attempt to disperse the crowd. I did nothing whatever to justify this brutal assault upon me by the police. I was never arrested in my life. I was not in the neighborhood while the riots were going on in the early part of the evening. The police did not give any reason for acting as they did, and when I fell unconscious they left me alone in the dark street.

HARRY S. CRAIG.

Sworn to before me this 13th day of September, 1900.

FRANK MOSS, Notary Public, N. Y. County.

City and County of New York, ss.:

John L. Newman, being duly sworn, deposes and says:

I reside at No. 351 West 37th Street, in the rear house. On August 15th, 1900, I went to the restaurant which is in the front building, for supper. This was about 10:30 P. M. After I had been there a few minutes some one told me that the mob was coming. I had seen them beat colored people during the evening, without any cause, so I walked out of the restaurant into my apartments, which are in the rear, only a few steps away; I live in the basement floor. I did this so as to avoid any trouble. As I reached the front door and walked in I closed it, and proceeded to go into my apartments. Four officers immediately came, and one of them said, "Stop!" and kicked open the door. Then one of them grabbed me and said, "Here is a d——d nigger; kill him!" The four officers then beat me with their clubs until I became unconscious. They then carried me to the station house. I was unconscious during all this time, but my friends tell me that the police were beating me all the way to the station house. It is located one block west from where I live. At the station house I recovered my consciousness. I was arraigned before the sergeant, and the officer who struck me first made the complaint against me. At the sergeant's desk I felt very weak, bleeding from my head and eye, and I held on to the railing for support. One of the officers struck me in the ribs with a night stick, and said, "God d—n you, stand up there!" I fell forward on the sergeant's desk, and I said, "For God's sake, take a gun and blow out my brains! If you have got to take a life, take mine, and don't murder me this way!" The sergeant then said very gruffly to the officer, "Take him away!" While all this was going on Chief of Police Devery was in the station house standing about ten feet away, talking to somebody whom I did not know. He saw all this, but did not interfere, conversing with the man all the time, as if nothing unusual was going on. I have known Chief Devery for three or four years, and have spoken with him in a friendly way many times. When I was brought into the muster room, in the rear of the station house, I saw several colored people being treated for their wounds. I was bleeding from my head and eye, and could not see well, and I sat down in the wrong chair. Two policemen then came over to me, pulled me out of the chair, and were raising their clubs to strike me when some one said, "Don't hit this man any more," and they obeyed. My wounds were then dressed, and I was taken to a cell. About twelve o'clock, when the officer who was making the prison rounds came to my cell, I asked him for permission to see the sergeant. He asked why, and I told him that my house was unlocked, and that I wished he would send an officer to lock it. He said he would speak to the sergeant about it. In a few minutes he returned and said, "The sergeant said, 'D—n him,' and that 'he had no business with the house,'" and he did not send anyone to lock it and protect my property. While I was in the station house I saw a colored man, John Haines, struck by several officers with their clubs. He was naked, only wearing a little undershirt. The officers were striking all the colored men in the station house, and without any interference. In court, the next morning, I was arraigned before Judge Cornell. The officer swore that I was causing a riot in the street, I denied this. I did not have any witnesses in court, because I did not have any opportunity to produce them. The Judge did not ask me whether I wanted an examination or not, and expressed his doubts as to my guilt, and said the case was "very curious." But the officers were persistent in their false statements, aforesaid, and the magistrate put me under $100 bonds to keep the peace. Not being able to furnish this, I was sent to the Penitentiary, where I was for thirty days. I was treated at the Penitentiary by Dr. Thomas Higgins, who told me that my head would never be right as long as I lived. I have been sick ever since. Dr. Higgins told me that he would testify for me in any proceeding which I might institute. I am employed by the Metropolitan Street Railway Company as a rockman, but am unable to work at present. I have lived in New York City for over forty-three years, and have never been arrested before in my life. I did not participate in the riots, was not on the street, and did nothing whatever to justify this conduct on the part of the police. I can recognize the officer who made the charge against me; he was the first to strike me.

JOHN L. NEWMAN.

Sworn to before me this 19th day of September, 1900.

JOHN F. MACCOLGAN, Notary Public (4), N. Y. County.

(The officer in the case was Holland.)

City and County of New York, ss.:

Mrs. Martha A. Brown, being duly sworn, deposes and says:

I reside at No. 351 West 37th Street. On Wednesday, August 15th, 1900, about 10:15 P. M., while on my way upstairs I saw John Newman, who lives in the rear house at the above number, come in the front door and close it; he had almost reached the rear of the hall when the front door was opened by a policeman who had his club raised, and who ran up to the said Newman, struck him over the head with his club, felling him to the floor; he then dragged Newman to the street, clubbing him meanwhile, and at the front door he was joined by four other officers, who assisted him to drag Newman out into the street, where they threw him into the midst of the mob which had congregated outside, and some of whom jumped on Newman, stamping on his stomach with their feet. Newman was then again taken by the officers and dragged to the station house on the next block. Deponent states further that Newman did not appear to be trying to get away from anyone, when he entered the front door, and further when he was struck first he was struck from behind.

MARTHA A. BROWN.

Sworn to before me this 24th day of September, 1900.

GEO. P. HAMMOND, JR., Notary Public (164), N. Y. County.

City and County of New York, ss.:

Mrs. Betty Green, being duly sworn, deposes and says:

I reside at No. 353 West 37th Street, Manhattan Borough, New York City. On Wednesday, August 15th, 1900, about eleven P. M., I saw John Newman coming out of the restaurant next door, No. 351, and spoke a few words to him, and saw him go into the hall door of the house in the rear of which he lived. Almost immediately I saw two officers in uniform, and about three others in citizens' clothes. The two in uniform ran into the hallway after the said John Newman, some of the officers saying, "Get the black son of a b——, and kill him!" Shortly afterward I saw the two men in uniform drag Newman out onto the stoop, clubbing him meanwhile. He sank to the stoop and lay there for some time. While he lay there a patrol wagon went by, and the officers tried to get it to stop; but it went on. They then took Newman and led him on down towards the station house. All the way to 9th Avenue every officer they met took a crack at him. Deponent states that Newman was perfectly sober, and had done nothing from the time that he left the restaurant till the officers ran after him into the hallway. She saw him make no resistance after the officers got him and clubbed him.

BETTY GREEN.

Sworn to before me this 27th day of September, 1900.

GEO. P. HAMMOND, JR., Notary Public (164), N. Y. County.

City and County of New York, ss.:

Miss Albertha L. Clark, being duly sworn, deposes and says:

I reside at No. 351 West 37th Street. On Wednesday, August 15th, 1900, between eleven and ten o'clock P. M., while looking out of the front window of my home, I saw an officer strike a colored man over the head with his club, and the man ran down towards my home, in front of which another officer hit him over the head with his club, and still another officer kicked him; then two officers took him to the station house. While this was going on I heard a noise in the hall, and in a few minutes I saw a colored man dragged from the hallway of my home, whom I recognized as John Newman, who lived in the rear house; the officers threw him into the mob, whereupon I left the window to see what had become of my folks, and when I returned to the window the officers were dragging Newman to the station house. After the above occurrence officers came through 37th Street from 8th Avenue, and ordered people who were sitting at the windows to go away from there, and without giving them sufficient time to do so drew their revolvers and fired them at the occupants of the windows.

ALBERTHA L. CLARK.

Sworn to before me this 24th day of September, 1900.

GEO. P. HAMMOND, JR., Notary Public (164), N. Y. County.

City and County of New York, ss.:

Mrs. Lucinda Thomson, being duly sworn, deposes and says:

I reside at No. 351 West 37th Street. On Wednesday, August 15th, 1900, I was at home and in my rooms between the hours of ten and eleven P. M. I have heard the statements given by my two daughters, namely, Albertha L. Clark and Mrs. Martha A. Brown, and have heard read the affidavits made and subscribed to by them, and I know of my own knowledge that all the facts therein stated are true.

her
MRS. LUCINDA x THOMSON.
mark

Sworn to before me this 24th day of September, 1900.

GEO. P. HAMMOND, JR., Notary Public (164), N. Y. County.

City and County of New York, ss.:

Mrs. Elizabeth Brown, being duly sworn, deposes and says:

I reside at No. 458 Seventh Avenue, New York City. On Saturday, August 18th, 1900, my brother, Charles A. Mitchell, twenty-seven years of age, and employed as a waiter, had heard of the riots and was on his way to see me, and had reached the corner of 34th Street and 7th Avenue, when he saw a mob of about five hundred people, led by eight or nine officers, who upon seeing him attacked and clubbed him, hitting him on the head and shoulders. He managed to reach the front door of my home and run into it, where I aided him and put him on a lounge; this was about ten o'clock on Saturday evening. His wife came to see him about 10:30 and took him home about one o'clock Sunday morning, where he stayed until about two A. M., when he became violent, and it became necessary to send him to the insane pavilion of Bellevue Hospital. All the time he was shouting in his delirium, "Devery did it! Devery did it! Here they come!" Deponent declares that while in the insane pavilion of Bellevue Hospital her brother, the said Charles A. Mitchell, was beaten and maltreated by the attendants thereat, he having a gash in his head about three inches long, and similar cuts on his wrist and two on his leg. He stayed at Bellevue from Sunday, the 19th of August, 1900, to Thursday, the 23rd of August, 1900, when he was removed to Ward's Island Insane Asylum. Deponent states further that her brother is of very slight build, being only five feet six inches in height and weighing about one hundred and twelve pounds, and that she witnessed the clubbing of her brother by the police as she was looking out of the front window at the time, and that the said clubbing was unjustifiable and brutal, and wholly without cause.

MRS. ELIZABETH BROWN.

Sworn to before me this 20th day of September, 1900.

GEO. P. HAMMOND, JR., Notary Public (164), N. Y. County.

City and County of New York, ss.:

Mrs. Elizabeth Brown, being duly sworn, deposes and says:

On Saturday, August 18th, 1900, I saw the mob going towards 37th Street, and while watching them I saw a colored man come up from a house somewhere on 7th Avenue between 36th and 37th Streets and run toward 35th Street. Some of the officers saw him and ran after him, catching him and clubbing him, leaving him lying on the car track for dead. He was picked up by some men and taken to a saloon on the northeast corner of 36th Street and 7th Avenue.

MRS. ELIZABETH BROWN.

Sworn to before me this 20th day of September, 1900.

GEO. P. HAMMOND, JR., Notary Public (164), N. Y. County.

City and County of New York, ss.:

Willis King, being duly sworn, deposes and says:

I reside at 346 West 41st Street, New York City. On Wednesday. August 15th, 1900, while passing through 34th Street, about 11:30 P. M., I was joined by a crowd of men and boys. I crossed over to the north side of the street, to where about a dozen officers stood, on the northeast corner, in front of a saloon. I was grabbed by three of them as soon as I got near them, and without saying a word they started me up 8th Avenue towards the station house. On the way up 8th Avenue the officer who was behind me, and who was feeling my clothes and pockets for weapons, said, "He has nothing." Whereupon the officer on my right suggested that they go down a dark street, which was done by turning west on 35th Street. We had gone about one third of the way down the block, on the south side of the street, when all three officers turned on me and beat me with their clubs over the head and body. I was felled to the sidewalk. When they stopped one of them remarked. "I guess that will do him for a while," whereupon all three of them walked off, leaving me lying upon the sidewalk. I managed to get to No. 327 West 35th Street, when a lady by the name of Mrs. Smith, who lives on the second floor, and who had seen the officers clubbing some one, was standing on the front stoop of her home; she asked me when she saw me whether it was I that had been clubbed, and I told her that it was. She then took me into Mrs. Conner's apartments on the first floor and dressed the cuts in my head. Deponent declares that he did not know anything about a disturbance, that he did not resist arrest, and that he was perfectly sober and on his way home from visiting a friend on East 27th Street.

WILLIS KING.

Sworn to before me this 27th day of September, 1900.

GEO. P. HAMMOND, JR., Notary Public (164). N. Y. County.

City and County of New York, ss.:

Isaiah O. Ferguson, being duly sworn, deposes and says:

I reside at 165 East 97th Street, New York City. On Wednesday evening, August 15th, 1900, I started to go downtown on the West Side, and had reached the neighborhood of 8th Avenue and 43rd Street, riding on an 8th Avenue car, which was of the combination type, and I was in the closed part, when I reached the aforementioned place. I noticed a large crowd of people, and patrol wagons and ambulances. I inquired from a gentleman who sat next to me what was the matter, and he replied that he did not know. We proceeded downtown and had reached the neighborhood of 36th Street, when suddenly the car, which had been proceeding very slowly, came to a dead stop. The motorman and the conductor both folded their arms and looked at me. The next I knew a number of men jumped on the car, some coming through the windows, and commenced beating me, and continued to beat me until I was insensible. When I came to, the car had started and was going slowly. I was bewildered and dazed, and I rushed from the car and downtown, several people on the way trying to stop me, but I was crazed with pain and fled on, until I was met by a lady friend, who stopped me on seeing my condition, and took me to her home, on 17th Street near 9th Avenue, where she bathed my head and dressed my wounds, and where I stayed until the next morning, when I went to Washington, D. C., where a physician attended to me. Deponent further states as the car stopped he noticed four police officers on the east side of the avenue, and that they made no attempt whatever to interfere with the mob: further, that he was proceeding on his journey in a quiet manner, and had not heard of any trouble, and that he had given absolutely no cause for the attack.

I. O. FERGUSON.

Sworn to before me this 21st day of September, 1900.

GEO. P. HAMMOND, JR., Notary Public (164), N. Y. County.

City and County of New York, ss.:

Headly Johnson, being duly sworn, deposes and says: I reside at 330 West 53rd Street. I am employed as a Pullman car porter, on the cars running out of the West Shore depot, Weehawken, N. J. I arrived on my train at the said depot on Thursday, August 16th, 1900, at 2:25 P. M. I arrived in New York about 5:30 P. M. the same day, and, having heard of the riots, I had prepared to protect myself from the mob by carrying home with me a revolver. I boarded a car at the West Shore ferry at the foot of West 42nd Street and transferred to an 8th Avenue car at 34th Street, and had proceeded as far as 40th Street, when the car was assailed by a mob shouting, "There's another nigger! Kill him! lynch him!" I stood up and was ready to defend myself, when a passenger on the car asked me to sit down, saying that if the mob got on the car he would help me defend myself. I sat down as requested, and happening to look over my shoulder I saw three police officers in uniform running after the car. They boarded the car, and, seizing me, one of the officers put his hand in my pocket and took the revolver from me, then pulled me off the car, saying, "Come off of here, you black son of a b———!" When they had pulled me off the car they immediately commenced clubbing me, and continued to do so all the way to the station house. While in the station house I saw several colored men beaten by police officers. The sergeant at the desk, when I was sent to a cell, shouted to the police officers, "Don't hit this man!" repeating the same several times. I was taken to the police court the next day, where I was discharged. Deponent states further that the officer who arrested him and appeared against him in the police court is the one who did the most of the clubbing; in fact, all of it except one blow. Deponent declares further that he was proceeding quietly to his home, where he was determined to go, and was not molesting anyone, and that when the officers signified their intention to arrest him he made no show of resistance, and that therefore the clubbing was unjustifiable and an outrage.

HEADLY JOHNSON.

Sworn to before me this 8th day of September, 1900.

GEO. P. HAMMOND, JR., Notary Public (164), N. Y. County.

City and County of New York, ss.:

Benjamin McCoy, being duly sworn, deposes and says: I reside at 226 West 40th Street. On Thursday, August 16th, 1900, about five A. M., I arose to go to my work. I went to Dobbins' restaurant, on 8th Avenue between 40th and 41st Streets, and had breakfast, after finishing which I went to the corner of 41st Street to board an 8th Avenue car, to reach my place of business. As I was standing waiting for the car I saw two officers walking on the east side of the street, and a colored man came running along with blood streaming from his head, and said to me, "Don't stand there; go away, or those policemen will club you to death; they just clubbed me." The car came along just then, and I walked out to get on board, and had put my hand on the rail, when one of the officers who had been on the other side of the street came suddenly around from behind the car, and struck me on the shin of my left leg, and struck me several times on the upper part of the leg, saying, "Get in there, get in there! What are you standing around here whistling for?" Deponent declares that he was not creating any disturbance at the time, and that there were not over four or five persons, outside of the police officers, on the street in the immediate neighborhood, and that the assault was entirely unwarranted and unjustifiable and a flagrant outrage, perpetrated, by one by whom deponent would expect, and had a right to expect, to be protected.

BENJAMIN MCCOY.

Sworn to before me this 7th day of September, 1900.

City and County of New York, ss.:

Albert Saunders, being duly sworn, deposes and says: I live at 440 West 45th Street. I work at 118 West 27th Street. On August 15th I left my work at night and walked up 8th Avenue toward my home. About 38th Street a crowd ran at me, somebody struck me, and I staggered, and then I received another blow that cut open my head and made me speechless. I found myself in the hands of an officer, who took me to the station house, where my wound was dressed. I stayed there till about four A. M. A number of colored men were brought in by officers, some of them cut and bleeding, like myself. I remember a colored man who was brought in bleeding, and naked except for a merino shirt. When he was taken back to the cells the policeman who had him clubbed his legs. Another man who had a cut head was advised by the jailer to put his head under the hydrant, but the man said he was afraid the officer who had him would strike him again if he got his head down, so the jailer got a pail and washed it. I was not in a position where I could see clearly all that happened, but I saw several other colored men struck and abused by policemen. I am an English subject, was born in St. Kitts, and suppose that my speech showed that I was not an American and protected me.

ALBERT SAUNDERS.

Sworn to before me this 5th day of September, 1900.

FRANK MOSS, Notary Public, N. Y. County.

City and County of New York, ss.:

George White, of 145 West 32nd Street, being duly sworn, deposes and says that on Wednesday, August 15th, 1900, at half past ten P. M., while riding on a 34th Street car, going east, he saw and heard a crowd of boys and young men running and yelling at the car that he was on, and that immediately after he saw three police officers board the said car, and upon seeing deponent they grabbed him by the arm and clubbed him over the head and arms, pulled him off the car, and continued to club him. They then took him to the West 37th Street station house, where his wounds were dressed by a surgeon from one of the hospitals, who was there. Deponent further states that he is not addicted to the use of liquor, had not been drinking on the said day, and that he was not intoxicated at the time of the clubbing; that he was not placed under arrest, and that he remained in the station house until after the storm came up, or as near as he can remember about three o'clock A. M. the next morning, by reason of being told that there was a mob outside waiting to beat all Negroes that they could catch. Further, that by reason of the suddenness of the attack he did not look closely at the assailants, so as to be able to identify them.

his
GEORGE x WHITE.
mark

Sworn to before me this 28th day of August, 1900.

GEO. P. HAMMOND, JR., Notary Public (164), N. Y. County.

City and County of New York, ss.:

Charles Bennett, being duly sworn, deposes and says:

I reside at No. 309 West 37th Street. On August 15th, 1900, I was working for a man named Mr. O'Connor, who keeps a saloon at Coney Island. I quit work at one o'clock A. M. the next day (August 16th), and started for home with a man named Wilson. We boarded an 8th Avenue car at Warren Street and Broadway, which was going north; just before we reached the street whereon I reside the conductor of the car upon which we were riding told us that there had been a riot, that it was because of the death of the police officer, and that they were attacking every colored man that they caught. I then said that we had better get off; the conductor then said that it was "pretty quiet" when he came down. We got off the car at 8th Avenue and 37th Street, and at 3:30 A. M. had almost reached the front door of my home when several police officers from among a group of about a dozen called to me asking me where I was going. I told them, "Home here." I was then in front of my door, and immediately after making my reply an officer hit me with his club, knocking me down. I struggled to my feet and endeavored to run towards 8th Avenue, but was pursued by the officers and knocked down again at the corner of 8th Avenue and 36th Street. It was raining very hard at the time, and they threw me into the gutter, which was full of rain water; they kept my head in the water until I strangled, when they let up, jumped on me, and pushed me back again into the gutter. After a while they called a patrol wagon, into which they threw me, and beat me all the way to the station house in 37th Street. Upon my arrival there my head had been cut open; I was covered with blood and bruises from the beating and clubbing I had received. While in the station house I told Captain Cooney that I had been clubbed by policemen. I remained in the station house for about half an hour, and while there I heard a man who was dressed in citizen's clothes say to the officers present, "Club every d——d nigger you see; kill them; shoot them; be brave, the same as I was." The man answered, "All right; will you stick to us?" He answered, "Yes, I'll stand by you." I heard this man called Thompson by some of the officers. He went among the colored men who were present and who were in almost as bad condition as I was, asking their names, where they had lived, and what they had been doing. After receiving their answers he said to each of them, "Get ter h——l home out of here; they'd ought ter have killed yer!" When he came to me he said, "What's your name?" I told him; then he said, "What were you doing?" I said, "I just come from work at Coney Island." He exclaimed, "Coney Island, eh! That's a d——d nice place to be working. Where do you live?" I told him, when he said, "Another nice place right in my district, the worst block in the whole district." He did not tell me to get out, but I was shortly after taken to Roosevelt Hospital and from there to Bellevue Hospital, where I remained a week, when I was taken to 54th Street Court, where I had a hearing and was discharged on August 28th, 1900. While I was being clubbed in the street one of the officers said, "Search him," whereupon they stopped the clubbing long enough to search my pockets and take fourteen dollars in bills from me, which I had in my hip pocket of my trousers. I have never had the said money returned to me. While I was in the station house Captain Cooney was there, but not in uniform, and the aforesaid man whom they called Thompson was giving orders to the men, in the presence of Captain Cooney. At the time that I had reached my home on the said night there was no disturbance in the neighborhood, and there was but one man in sight, and he was chased away by the officers. Everything was quiet in the neighborhood, and on the way uptown on the car I saw no signs of a disturbance, and would not have known anything about there having been anything of the kind if I had not been informed by the car conductor. I can identify two of the officers who took part in the clubbing, one of whom was dressed in citizen's clothes, and who, I think, was one of the wardmen attached to that precinct. (The witness subsequently identified Officer Herman Ohm.) Deponent further states that he has resided in the City of New York for the past fifteen years, and has never been arrested before in his life, and has always been a quiet, law-abiding citizen.

his
CHARLES x BENNETT.
mark

Sworn to before me this 31st day of August, 1900.

GEO. P. HAMMOND, JR., Notary Public (164), N. Y. County.

City and County of New York, ss.:

James Joseph Lockett, being duly sworn, deposes and says:

I reside at No. 323 West 37th Street, in the Borough of Manhattan. I am a cigar maker, and am employed by Gahio & Roverie, on East 37th Street. On Wednesday, August 15th, 1900, at about eight P. M., accompanied by my wife, I called at the residence of Thomas H. McGuire, a friend of mine who resides at No. 410 West 36th Street, where we remained until about 11:15 P. M. We walked east on 36th Street to 8th Avenue, where we met four police officers in uniform on the northwest corner. We passed them and turned into 8th Avenue, walking on the west side of the avenue, towards 37th Street. We had not gone over fifty feet when the officers ran after us and beat us with their clubs. One of the officers said to me. "You black son of a b——, you have a knife!" and struck me on the head with a club several times, and then led us to the station house. There we were searched by the officer, who took eleven dollars in money—two two-dollar bills, one five-dollar bill, and two one-dollar bills—one rent receipt for thirteen dollars and fifty cents for August, signed by Herbert Peck & Co., none of which has been returned to me. The sergeant, in uniform, was behind the desk, and the roundsman made the entry. I was charged with being drunk and carrying a knife. My head was bleeding profusely from the wounds inflicted by the police officers, and the police surgeon at the station house had to dress them. After this I was placed in a cell. The next morning I was arraigned in the Magistrates' Court on West 54th Street. The officer swore that I was drunk and disorderly and carried a knife. The magistrate held me in $500 bail, and I was bailed by Mr. Garner. I was not drunk on the occasion in question. I had drunk three, and positively not more than four, glasses of beer at Mr. McGuire's house. I did nothing which would justify this conduct on the part of the police officers. On August 23rd an officer called at my house. He said he was generally known as "Bootsey," and was sent by the Captain to obtain a statement from me, which I gave him. He was in citizen's clothes. He called again on August 24th, and said that Captain Cooney wanted to see me at the station house. I did not go to see him.

JAMES JOSEPH LOCKETT.

Sworn to before me this 28th day of August, 1900.

STEPHEN B. BRAGUE, Notary Public (125), N. Y. County.

City and County of New York, ss.:

Lavinia Lockett, being duly sworn, deposes and says:

That she is the wife of James Joseph Lockett, and resides at 323 West 37th Street, in the Borough of Manhattan. That on August 15th, 1900, at about eight o'clock in the evening, she with her husband visited Mr. Thomas H. McGuire, a friend of ours, where we remained until about 11:15 P. M. Walking easterly to 8th Avenue, we met four police officers in uniform on the northwest corner. We had gone about fifty feet, when the officers ran after us and struck my husband with a club and said, "You black son of a b———, you have a knife," and when deponent screamed she was struck in the mouth and chest with a club by one of the officers. We were taken to the station and locked in cells; my husband was charged with being drunk and disorderly, and we were held in bail in the sum of $500. Neither my husband nor myself was intoxicated, and saw no crowd or any row and no excitement on our way home until we were assaulted.

LAVINIA LOCKETT.

Sworn to before me this 28th day of August, 1900.

STEPHEN B. BRAGUE, Notary Public (125), N. Y. County.

City and County of New York, ss.:

William Hamer, of No. 494 7th Avenue, being duly sworn, deposes and says:

I am a musician. I am employed at "The Fair," kept by Mr. Samuels, on 14th Street between 3rd and 4th Avenues. My wife is employed there also. On August 15th I finished my work about 11:30 P. M. I took the crosstown 14th Street car and changed to the 7th Avenue horse cars. I had not heard anything of the riot. The car stopped between 36th and 37th Streets, and my wife and I were dragged from the car by a crowd of men and lads armed with sticks and stones. I ran into a stable at 37th Street and 7th Avenue, and they beat me in there and left me for dead. A stone or something hit me in the stomach, and I fell into a water trough. My wife and I were separated, and she did not find me. I crawled out of the stable into a lumber yard and lay there in my blood until three A. M. I have been in the doctor's care ever since, and am out to-day for the first time. My doctor is Dr. Yarnell, of Park Avenue near 84th Street. When I was pulled out of the car I noticed a colored man lying unconscious on the ground. There were at least a dozen policemen standing around. They did nothing, and made no effort to protect me.

WILLIAM HAMER.

Sworn to before me this 31st day of August, 1900.

FRANK MOSS, Notary Public, N. Y. County.

City and County of New York, ss.:

Mrs. Annie Hamer, being duly sworn, deposes and says that she resides at 494 7th Avenue; that she is employed as a musician at "The Fair," in East 14th Street; that on Wednesday, August 15th, 1900, about midnight thereof, she in company with her husband arrived at 7th Avenue between 36th and 37th Streets on a 7th Avenue car; that when she alighted from the car she found herself surrounded by a mob, and almost instantly was struck in the mouth with a brick, thrown by some one whom she does not know. She became separated from her husband, and did not know what became of him until three A. M. the next morning, when he came home all covered with blood. Deponent states further that she has read the affidavit of her husband, hereto attached, and knows of her own knowledge that the facts therein stated are true. Deponent further states that she has been informed by her mother that the "captain" stationed officers at the door of her residence, and told them to "not let anyone in or out, and if anyone attempted it to shoot them."

ANNIE HAMER.

Sworn to before me this 6th day of September, 1900.

GEO. P. HAMMOND, JR., Notary Public (164), N. Y. County.

City and County of New York, ss.:

William Lemoine, residing at 68 West 43rd Street, being duly sworn, deposes and says that on Wednesday, August 15th, 1900, he started at 7:55 P. M. to attend a meeting of Odd Fellows being held at 29th Street between 6th and 7th Avenues, and had reached 7th Avenue between 35th and 36th Streets, when he met two white men, who said to him, "You had better not go down that way, you will get mobbed." I said, "Mobbed! for what?" They said, "Why, they are having a riot down there." I continued on, however, until I reached 34th and 35th Streets on 7th Avenue, where I met two white women, who said to me, "Do you want to get killed? If you don't you had better go on back." I thereupon went no further in that direction, but turned back up 7th Avenue, and went as far as 483 7th Avenue, and saw a crowd coming down 7th Avenue from about 41st Street, and another from about 34th Street. Both of the crowds were composed of boys and young men who were in the lead shouting and yelling, while in the midst of them were two or three police officers. The boys would stir up a colored man and begin yelling, "There he goes! There is one of them!" and the boys would immediately run after them, and the police follow. I saw them overtake two colored men, and saw the police take them down 37th Street towards 8th Avenue. While I was standing in front of 483 7th Avenue a friend of mine, Mrs. Harriet Ann Bruna, who now resides at 152 West 27th Street, called to me from her window, and told me to come upstairs, which I did. She then said that I had better go into the hall bedroom and stay there overnight, as I might get hurt if I stayed outside or attempted to get home. This was about 8:30 P. M. I then went into the hall bedroom aforementioned, and remained there looking out of the window for about one hour and a half, during which time the blinds were closed or turned down; I then undressed and went to bed, and was in bed about an hour and three quarters, or until about 11:45 P. M., when I heard a crash at the front door downstairs and heard some one coming upstairs; when they reached my door they knocked at it with their clubs, and broke in the central panel of the door, when I said, "Don't break in the door, gentlemen; I'll open it," which I did. Four officers in uniform and two men in citizens' clothes came in, and exclaimed, "Here is the d——d nigger; kill him!" One in citizen's clothes came over to me (I had fallen on the bed) and, striking me on the hip with his club, said, "Come, get up out of there, where is that gun?" I said, "I have no gun; there's my clothes; search them and the room. I have done nothing; I have been asleep." The officers then searched the room, my clothes, and myself, and found nothing. The one in citizen's clothes then said, "He has no gun; we can't do anything." The women in the house commenced to scream, and the officers then broke in the door of Mrs. Elizabeth Mitchell, on the second floor, frightening her so that she has been unable to leave her bed ever since. I was hipshodden for a couple of days, and I rubbed it with liniment for a couple of days until the misery got out of it. Deponent further says that he has resided in San Francisco for the past eight years, and had just arrived in the city the day before the riot, and did not create any disturbance at that or any other time; and further, that he did not fire any shot from any firearm on that evening; and furthermore, never owned a gun, and never carried one.

WILLIAM LEMOINE.

Sworn to before me this 30th day of August, 1900.

GEO. P. HAMMOND, JR., Notary Public (164), N. Y. County.

City and County of New York, ss.:

Walter W. Coulter (white), 481 7th Avenue, being duly sworn, deposes and says that on Wednesday evening, August 15th, 1900, there was quite a disturbance around his place of business, and at about 11:30 P. M. he saw a number of officers and men in citizens' clothes go into the houses 481 and 483, and he, thinking they were part of the crowd of roughs, stepped up to a police officer, who was quite tall and stout and of reddish complexion, and said to him, "Why do you allow those rowdies to go up into that house; there is no one except a lot of respectable women and children in there, and possibly one man." The police officer replied as follows: "You go on and mind your own respectability, and you will have enough to do; they just shied a brick at us." Deponent further states that no brick had been thrown; that, in fact, they could not get a brick, as he was looking for one a short while before that to do some repairing with, and could not find one; that the only apparent reason for their going into the house was the fact that a large, tall man, whom he can identify if he sees him again, came along 7th Avenue, and seeing this colored man in the window called out, "There's a big nigger; get him!" and immediately there was a rush made for the house. Deponent states further that the police knew there were none but respectable people in that house, as deponent had gone to a great deal of trouble to get rid of a lot of dissolute people who were in the house about a year ago, and in his endeavors to get rid of them had called upon the police to aid him, so that they were perfectly cognizant of the facts in the case.

WALTER W. COULTER.

Sworn to before me this 31st day of August, 1900.

GEO. P. HAMMOND, JR., Notary Public (164), N. Y. County.

City and County of New York, ss.:

Mrs. Elizabeth Mitchell, being duly sworn, deposes and says that she resides at 481 7th Avenue; that on Wednesday evening, August 15th, 1900, about 11:30 P. M., two police officers in citizens' clothes and one in citizen's dress broke in the door of her apartments claiming to be looking for "the man that threw the bottle." She answered and said that "no bottle was thrown," and that it was a shame for them to break in the door of respectable people; that her sister, Mrs. Kate Jackson, became frightened at the uproar, and thinking that the life of her children and herself was in danger, jumped out of the window with her three-year-old child in her arms, thereby endangering the life of herself and child, and in consequence is now confined to her bed with shock, fright, and bruises. That at six A. M. the next morning she saw a colored man and woman assaulted on the corner of 36th Street and 7th Avenue. Also at 52nd Street and 7th Avenue, between eleven and twelve A. M., she saw a colored man assaulted by a white man, and when the officer attempted to interfere and arrest the white man the motormen around the stables refused to allow him to arrest him. She states further that one of the officers' first name was "Jim," as she heard him so addressed by the man in citizen's clothes.

MRS. ELIZABETH MITCHELL.

Sworn to before me this 31st day of August, 1900.

GEO. P. HAMMOND, JR., Notary Public (164), N. Y. County.

City and County of New York, ss.:

Mrs. Kate Jackson, being duly sworn, deposes and says that she resides at 481 7th Avenue, and that on Wednesday evening, August 15th, 1900, she heard a great commotion in the hallway and almost immediately a loud knocking on her door, and loud demands to open the door. She thought by the sound that the mob that she had heard and seen about the house was endeavoring to get into her rooms, and do her and her children bodily harm, and possibly murder. She caught up her youngest child (three years old) in her arms, and in her frenzy and fright jumped out the window on to a shed and thence to the yard, the child still in her arms, receiving bruises during her descent which have made her lame and unable to walk, and has suffered so from shock that she is now in bed and unable to leave it, and is under the care of her physician, Dr. William Hartley, 335 West 34th Street.

MRS. KATIE JACKSON.

Sworn to before me this 31st day of August, 1900.

GEO. P. HAMMOND, JR., Notary Public (164), N. Y. County.

City and County of New York, ss.:

William L. Hall, being duly sworn, deposes and says that he resides at 202 West 49th Street; that he is employed as an elevator conductor by R. H. Macy & Co., on West 14th Street; that on August 15th, 1900, he was on his way to visit a friend at 410 West 36th Street, and had reached 36th Street and 9th Avenue, when a crowd of young men and boys, from about sixteen to nineteen years of age, got around him and commenced yelling, jeering, hooting, and striking him with their fists, and with sticks, pieces of pipe, and one in particular struck him in the side with a weapon made of a long piece of wire, with a hammer head fastened to it. He ran away from the crowd, and succeeded in reaching a house in 36th Street between 8th and 9th Avenues, and succeeded in defending himself there for about an hour and a half, and finally managed to get out and home. Deponent states further that at the time of the assault, and at the commencement of it, four officers in full uniform were in the midst of the crowd of rioters, and were with them while they (the rioters) were attacking the house with stones, and that at that time, and at no time during the assault by the rioters, did these officers make any attempt to protect deponent, or to stop the assault by the rioters, but on the contrary, by reason of their presence and inaction on their part, they encouraged the said rioters to greater deeds of violence; that the deponent is a peaceable, law-abiding citizen and a member of St. Mark's M. E. Church, on West 53rd Street, and that on the said evening he was molesting no one, and was walking quietly along with Joseph Cæser, of 121 West 46th Street, and John Hansborough, of 329 West 53rd Street, who also were attacked by the rioters.

WILLIAM L. HALL.

Sworn to before me this 1st day of September, 1900.

GEO. P. HAMMOND, JR., Notary Public (164), N. Y. County.

City and County of New York, ss.:

William E. Johnson, being duly sworn, deposes and says:

I reside at 332 West 37th Street. On Wednesday, August 15th, 1900, fearing that there might be trouble over the killing of Officer Thorpe, I remained in the house all day and did not go out until about eleven P. M., when I went across the street to get my mail from 331 West 37th Street, where I have a letter box, because where I live at present the letter boxes are easily rifled, and this box is more secure. Upon returning to the house, which I did about five or ten minutes after leaving it, I found a police officer standing in the front of the house, ordering the tenants who were sitting on the front stoop to go inside, and saying that if he found them there when he came back he would club every one of them that he found there. The people then jumped up and ran inside, and the officer immediately followed them, striking at them, and struck one woman across the face. As the people got inside the vestibule door the said door closed, and I, thinking that the officer would not go inside, opened the door and stepped inside, whereupon the officer rushed into the hall, and struck me a blow on the head, felling me to my knees. I said, "Officer, I have done nothing; why do you strike me?" The officer said nothing, but jumped over me, chasing some of the tenants who had not succeeded in getting upstairs. While he was doing that I went out into the street, holding my head, which had been cut open by the blow, when the officer came out of the house and, grabbing me, pushed me into the street and commenced to club me again. I ran across the street to the tailor shop of I. Cohn, at 337 West 37th Street, and into the back room of his place, and fell on the sofa, where the officer, who had followed me in, renewed the clubbing and dragged me out into the street and to the 37th Street station house; and on the corner of 9th Avenue and 37th Street they met an officer who was in citizen's clothes. The said officer drew his billy from his pocket, and struck me a blow across the neck, and put his billy back into his pocket. When I reached the station house I did not answer any questions, and the sergeant who was behind the desk knew my last name and entered it on the blotter as Albert Johnson, not knowing my first name. I was put in a cell, and after I was put in a cell two more were put in with me, and once or twice while I was there an officer came through, and going to each cell called the occupant to the door, asked them their names, etc., and would then take his billy and push it through the bars into their faces. In one case he struck one man in the face, knocking out two of his front teeth; this man was sent to the island the next day, and I believe is now there. On the Tuesday following Acting Captain Cooney called and brought me down to the station house, and asked me who the officer was that assaulted me. Deponent then described the officer to him, and after consulting the blotter he handed me a slip of paper whereon was written the name "Herman Ohm" saying that was the name of the officer who had assaulted me. Captain Cooney expressed surprise that any of the officers should have beaten me, as I was known to a great many of them. The officer charged me with having a gun, and of giving him a fight in the hallway, but did not produce the gun and was given until the next day to produce it, when he produced a revolver and a bread knife of peculiar shape, claiming that was what I had in my possession at the time of my arrest. Deponent denied then and now that he had ever had a revolver and knife in his possession, and that the only thing that was found on him and taken from him was fifty cents in money and a small penknife. Notwithstanding the denial of the ownership of the revolver and knife by the deponent, and also that the officer brought no witnesses as to his taking the said articles from him, deponent was fined fifteen dollars, which was paid.

W. E. JOHNSON.

Sworn to before me this 4th day of September. 1900.

GEO. P. HAMMOND. JR., Notary Public (164), N. Y. County.

City and County of New York, ss.:

Edwin H. Broadard, being duly sworn, deposes and says that he resides at 332 West 37th Street; that he witnessed the action of the officer mentioned in the above affidavit of W. E. Johnson, and also the subsequent clubbing of Johnson by the said officer, and that deponent was one of the tenants who was chased off the stoop by the said officer; that the assault on the tenants by the said officer was unwarranted and without justification.

EDWIN H. BROADARD.

Sworn to before me this 4th day of September, 1900.

GEO. P. HAMMOND, JR., Notary Public (164), N. Y. County.

City and County of New York, ss.:

Mrs. Rosa Lewis, being duly sworn, deposes and says:

I reside at 332 West 37th Street. On Wednesday, August 15th, 1900, about eleven P. M., I in company with my husband and a number of other tenants were sitting on the front stoop of our home, when an officer approached and ordered us to "get inside out of that," adding that if we didn't he'd club us. All of the tenants immediately obeyed and passed on into the hallway, and I had reached the foot of the stairs leading up to my rooms when the officer, who had rushed into the hallway, struck me over the back with his club; I was lame in my back and suffered pain from it for a number of days. Deponent states further that the staircase is in the center of the house and about fifteen feet from the main entrance; that she was using every endeavor to comply with the command of the officer, which was given in an insulting and ill-natured manner.

ROSA LEWIS.

Sworn to before me this 13th day of September, 1900.

GEO. P. HAMMOND, JR., Notary Public (164), N. Y. County.

City and County of New York, ss.:

Maria Williams, of No. 206 West 27th Street, and Carrie Wells, of No. 239 West 29th Street, in the Borough of Manhattan, being severally duly sworn, depose and say:

On Wednesday, August 15th, 1900, we were sitting on the stoop of No. 239 West 29th Street, talking; we had been sitting there since 9:30 P. M. We had there learned of the assaults on the Negroes in this section, and heard the noise of the crowds and the stopping of the cars on 8th Avenue. There was no crowd in the street at this time. There were white and colored folks sitting on nearly all the stoops, the same as occurs on any ordinary warm night. About 11:30 several officers came through the street from 8th Avenue and walked towards 7th Avenue, three on the north side and four on the south side. No one in the street had been molested by anyone. These officers walked up the stoops, and without any warning ordered us into our houses, at the same time striking at us. Mrs. Wells, the mother of deponent Carrie Wells, was on the stoop one step from the bottom with three of her children, aged respectively fourteen, thirteen, and twelve years. An officer who is called "Joe," and whom we know, stepped up to Mrs. Wells, and said, "Get in there, you black son of a b———," and struck her viciously across the right hip, when she ran in with her children, the officers still following, striking at her until he reached the top step, looked around, and threatened to strike us if we came out again, and he then went away. Deponent Williams looked out of her window and saw these officers go through the same procedure wherever colored folks were sitting. Nothing was said or done to any white people. We see this officer every day. At about 2:15 in the morning some officers came through the block and clubbed colored people wherever they saw them, men as well as women. Deponent Wells lives at home with her mother, and helps her keep house; deponent Williams keeps house for herself and husband. Deponent Wells is a member of the Church of the Transfiguration, at 29th Street and 5th Avenue, where I have attended for years. Mr. and Mrs. Miller, of West 29th Street, know of us; Mrs. McGurk, of No. 225 West 29th Street, Mrs. Kloze, of 223 West 29th Street, all can vouch for our character.

CARRIE WELLS.
her
MARIA x WILLIAMS.
mark

Sworn to before me this 4th day of September. 1900.

SAMUEL MARCUS, Notary Public. N. Y. County.

City and County of New York, ss.:

Mrs. Irene Wells, being duly sworn, deposes and says that she resides at No. 239 West 29th Street; that on Wednesday evening, about nine o'clock P. M., she visited a sick friend, named Mrs. Twine (who has since died), at

No. 216 West 29th Street, and while there, and at about eleven o'clock P. M., hearing of the riot, she rushed out of said 216 West 29th Street to look for her children and get them safely at home—she having five children, and, motherlike, was anxious to get them out of danger. That while gathering her children together she noticed six police officers on each side of the street, and had succeeded in getting her children up the stoop and into the hallway of her home, and was on the second step of her stoop going upstairs, when Police Officer 1065 came along, and, striking her across the right hip with his club, said, "Get in out of here!" and made several passes at her, and pursued her up two or three steps of the stoop, but she rushed on up the stoop, driving her children before her, and escaped him and his blows. Deponent further says that she is a widow, and the sole support of her five children, by doing general housework, ironing, and washing, etc., and has done so for the past seven years; that she is a thoroughly respectable woman, and is peaceful and quiet at all times, and deems this assault by the police officer aforementioned an outrage, and without cause or provocation. There were three children on the stoop with her.

IRENE WELLS.

Sworn to before me this 31st day of August, 1900.

GEO. P. HAMMOND. JR., Notary Public (164), N. Y. County.

City and County of New York, ss.:

William H. Ross, being duly sworn, says:

I reside at 475 7th Avenue, near 36th Street, New York City. I had lived a short time at 225 West 32nd Street. I have lived for five years in New York. I have been a messenger for General Daniel E. Sickles. At about eleven o'clock on the evening of August 15th deponent was on his way to his rooms, but was stopped at Zion's flat and advised to come in and not cross the street, as there was a riot. I went in and went up two pair of stairs until about four o'clock in the morning, and slept on the stairs. My hour for going to work that morning was five o'clock, at the Herald Building, where I was working for Marsell, who attends to housecleaning and to the building. Another man, whose name I learned was Hicks, took refuge in the building at the same time. At about half past four o'clock on the morning of the 16th we heard a great commotion in the house. Three policemen rushed upstairs; the first one said, "You d——d black son of a b——, if you move I will shoot you like a dog!" He then hit me on the head with his club, and cut my head open; the other one then hit me on the head, and both beat me with their clubs on the neck, back, shoulders, chest, and ribs until I was bloody and sore and fell down, when one of the officers poked his pistol in my face and said, "You black son of a b——, just move or say a word, and I will shoot you like a cur." They also beat Hicks and broke his nose. People whom I did not know, looking out of windows, cried out about the brutality. They then had their fun with us, saying, "You d——d niggers; get out of here." Then when we would start they would again grab us, beat us, and threaten to shoot us. I would know one of these policemen, as I saw him since on 7th Avenue, and also in September at Broadway and 12th Street. I think that I would know the other fellow. In taking us to court they swore to the most outrageous lies, without any reason in fact. They stated we had been on the roof throwing bottles on the street. I had never been in the house in my life, never had been in a room and not above the second story, where they gave me shelter. The policemen told other lies—that they arrested me before, that he had warned me before on the street, that he had arrested me for fighting a few days before. The judge asked if they had any witnesses; they answered "Yes," and he gave them until three o'clock, when we were discharged. I was never arrested before in my life. Two doctors gave me certificates of character, which I had in court.

WILLIAM H. ROSS.

Sworn to before me this 4th day of September, 1900.

STEPHEN B. BRAGUE, Notary Public (125). N. Y. County.

City and County of New York, ss.:

Robert Myrick, being duly sworn, deposes and says that he resides at 414 West 39th Street, and is employed by Bernard Brennan, saloon keeper at 49th Street and Broadway; that on Thursday evening, August 16th, at about eight P. M., he left his work at the said saloon and walked to 8th Avenue between 47th and 48th Streets; that he entered a restaurant on that block, and after eating a meal he asked the proprietor whether there was any trouble downtown to-night. He replied, "No, it is kind of quiet to-night, but I guess you had better take a car and ride down, it will be safer." He replied. "I guess that will be the best way," and then walked out onto the avenue and boarded a car bound downtown, and had gone as far as 42nd Street when a mob of about one hundred boys, none of whom apparently were over nineteen years of age, began to throw stones at the car and yell, "There's a nigger in the car; let's kill him!" Some woman on the car said, "Come over here, mister; don't stand there and get killed." I went along the footboard from the rear of the car, where I had been, and got under the seat, where the mob could not see me; but the mob continued following the car and stoned it until I reached 39th Street, where I wanted to get off, but was advised there by three men (who were the only passengers that had remained on the car) not to get off. I continued on until the car reached 38th Street, when the car stopped and the mob caught up with it. I then got off the east side of the car, and ran over to the southeast corner of 8th Avenue, to where I saw five men standing, and going up to one I said, "Officer, will you please see me home?" He said, "Where do you live?" I told him. He then said, "What are you doing on the street at this time of night?" I answered, "Going home from work." He then asked me where I worked. I told him. He then said. "Have you got a gun or a razor?" I said "I have neither." He then proceeded to search me, when I remembered having a razor in a case in my outside coat pocket, and I told the officer and showed him where it was. He then took the razor out of my pocket, and, striking me across the back of the neck with his club, said, "You black son of a b——!" and then struck me several times on the head. I said to him, "I come over to you for protection, and this is what I get." He then said, "Shut up!" I was then taken to the 37th Street station house, and while there I was kicked by the officers in the section room, and by the doorman, and when I protested I was told to shut up. I was locked in cell No. 13, and in the morning I was brought to the 54th Street police court, where the judge turned me loose. While in my cell I got into conversation with a colored man who is a porter for the N. Y. C. & H. R. R., and he said that he was dragged from a street car and clubbed by police officers. Deponent further states that he had the aforementioned razor in his pocket by reason of the fact that it needed repairing, and he had taken it to a barber to see if he could fix it, and finding that he could not fix it he was taking it to his home to lay it away in its place. Deponent says further that the time of the clubbing was about 8:30 P. M.

ROBERT MYRICK.

Sworn to before me this 1st day of September, 1900.

GEO. P. HAMMOND, JR., Notary Public (164), N. Y. County.

City and County of New York, ss.:

Solomon Russell Wright, being duly sworn, deposes and says:

I reside at No. 129 West 27th Street; on Thursday, August 16th, 1900, about 6:30 P. M., I left the house and walked to the corner of 7th Avenue and 28th Street, where I met a friend of mine, with whom I stood and chatted for about three quarters of an hour, when I left and returned down 7th Avenue towards 27th Street, and had got within about one hundred feet of 27th Street, when I was struck by a missile thrown by an Italian boy. I naturally turned around and asked him what he had done that for. I passed on, however, and had got about fifty feet east of 7th Avenue, on 27th Street, when a police officer ran after me, and seizing me commenced feeling around my clothes as if in search of something. I had an ordinary pocket knife in the change pocket of my coat, and the officer finding it said, "What are you doing with this?" I answered, "Do you see me doing anything with it?" He then took me to the 30th Street station house (19th Precinct), and while going up the steps of the station house I stumbled, and the officer then hit me on the back of the neck with his club. I was arraigned before the sergeant, who took my pedigree, and at the close of that proceeding the officer who had me in charge, and whose name is Kennedy, said to the sergeant, "What will we do with this feller?" The sergeant replied, "Kill the black son of a b———!" The said officer then brought me back, and when we reached a flight of stairs leading down to the cells he shoved me down the whole flight; when I reached the bottom some other officers who were down there grabbed me and punched and beat me with their fists. I was arraigned the next day and charged with carrying a knife, and I was committed for ninety days. I served part of the time, when I was released on bail. I was not intoxicated, and had never been arrested before in my life. I never have and do not stand around the corners of the neighborhood; and further, I am employed by the Standard Oil Company as a porter.

SOLOMON R. WRIGHT.

Sworn to before me this 22nd day of September, 1900.

GEO. P. HAMMOND, JR., Notary Public (164). N. Y. County.

City and County of New York, ss.:

Alfred Bradshaw, being duly sworn, deposes and says:

I reside at No. 210 West 27th Street with my wife and three children. On August 16th, 1900, I bought a revolver on the Bowery, which I intended to take home in the evening and leave there, as a protection for my wife and children. There were numerous riots in the neighborhood the evening before, and the rioters had broken into houses at all times during the day and night, and I deemed it necessary for the protection of my wife and children. I had been working at 96 Greene Street that day. I am a general housecleaner, and work in all parts of the city. As I was walking home on 7th Avenue, about four o'clock in the afternoon, between 14th and 15th Streets, I saw a man run up to a police officer and say something to him. The officer then came up to me and said, "You've got a pistol; you give it up. I will arrest you." I handed him the pistol, and he arrested me. I said as I handed it to him, "I bought this pistol to protect my family at home. I heard of this rioting, and I bought this pistol to protect my home." He said, "Why don't you call to the officers for protection?" I said, "The officers can't protect my home, because I don't know what time the riot might come in, and we can't always find an officer on beat. I heard them break into some houses and beat people unmercifully." I was taken to the 30th Street station house. While there I saw Solomon Wright, who is at present in the Penitentiary at Blackwell's Island, a Negro, being clubbed by a policeman as he was being led from the sergeant's desk into the cell. He was bleeding from his head, and his eye was discolored. I have been in the city for twenty years, and have never been arrested before. I did not show this pistol to anyone after I bought it, and intended to leave it at the house, as a protection to my family.

his
ALFRED x BRADSHAW.
mark

Sworn to before me this 4th day of September, 1900.

STEPHEN B. BRAGUE. Notary Public (125), N. Y. County.

City and County of New York, ss.:

John H. Kellum, being duly sworn, deposes and says:

I was on a Broadway car on the evening of Wednesday, August 15th, at about 11:30 P. M. I boarded the car at the corner of 46th Street and Broadway, and had reached a point a little north of 35th Street, when I heard a mob run after the car and commence throwing missiles at and into the car. Among other missiles was a little bottle, which I caught, and with which I kept the rioters at bay. The car got a short distance ahead of the mob, when it had passed 34th Street, and I took advantage of that and jumped from the car and ran towards three policemen in uniform, and two who were in citizens' clothes. One of them said not to run any further, and one of the men in citizens' clothes said, "Get on this car, and I'll get on with you." I did so and rode to 32nd Street, and the said officer got on the rear platform of the same car. I got off at 32nd Street and was not molested again. Deponent further says that the officers made no attempt to disperse the mob, though they were in plain sight. Deponent further says that he has lived in the 19th Precinct for about eighteen years, and is well known to a number of the officers of that precinct.

J. H. KELLUM.

Sworn to before me this 7th day of September, 1900.

GEO. P. HAMMOND, JR., Notary Public (164), N. Y. County.

(This was in the 19th, not the 20th Precinct.)

City and County of New York, ss.:

Samuel Isaiah Johnson, being duly sworn, deposes and says:

I reside at No. 125 West 27th Street, in the Borough of Manhattan, and support myself by cleaning carpet, chimney sweeping, and other jobs of a like nature. I have been employed by a Mr. Webb, an attorney with an office near Jefferson Market; a Mr. Davis, proprietor of a fish market there; Mr. Andrew Phillips, 15th Street and 6th Avenue. On Wednesday. August 15th, 1900, the first night of the riots, I was on an 8th Avenue car bound south. I had been up to see my brother-in-law, Joseph W. Brown, of No. 85 West 104th Street. I had my banjo with me. I left there shortly after nine. He was out. About ten o'clock, at about 41st Street and 8th Avenue, a crowd jumped on the car, grabbed me, and tried to pull me out of the car. I was under the seat. They took my banjo, hat, coat, and belt away, and beat me all over the body and head, so that I was unable to move. The car was at a standstill while I was being beaten, which lasted from about fifteen to twenty minutes. Another colored man was being beaten at the same time. After about twenty minutes of this a man, probably a detective, jumped on the car, and the crowd allowed the car to proceed. He took me to the corner of 27th Street and 7th Avenue, and asked me whether I could get home, and he left me. I proceeded to my house unmolested. The next day I went to the hospital at 15th Street and 5th Avenue, and obtained some liniment for my bruises. I am fifty-four years of age, small in stature, and lame.

his
SAMUEL x ISAIAH JOHNSON.
mark

Sworn to before me this 6th day of September, 1900.

SAMUEL MARCUS, Notary Public, N. Y. County.

City and County of New York, ss.:

Thomas Hughes (white), of No. 646 East 13th Street, New York City, being duly sworn, deposes and says:

On August 15th, 1900 (the first day of the outbreak), about 8:45 P. M., I was in 36th Street between 7th and 8th Avenues. I was on my way home after having called on Rev. Leighton Williams, at 312 West 54th Street. There were quite a number of persons moving about in the street, and half a dozen policemen moving about. I noticed a colored man about five feet seven, smooth-faced, about twenty-eight or thirty years old, standing in front of a doorway near a grocery store. He wasn't doing anything, and wasn't talking to anybody. An officer with a heavy reddish mustache rushed across the street at him and said, "You black bastard, what are you doing here?" and at the same instant struck him over the head with his club, felling the Negro to the street. The Negro bled and lay unconscious. I tried to wipe the blood from him, and the officer spoke roughly to me and ordered me away. Friends of the Negro dragged him into the hallway. My journey was down 8th Avenue to 36th Street, and down 7th Avenue to 35th Street, and I saw a number of police officers strike a number of persons with their clubs. All whom I saw struck were colored persons, and I noticed that as a peculiar fact. I was accompanied by William Shea, of 332 East 23rd Street.

THOMAS HUGHES.

Sworn to before me this 30th day of September, 1900.

FRANK MOSS, Notary Public, N. Y. County.

City and County of New York, ss.:

William Shea, of 332 East 23rd Street, being duly sworn, deposes and says:

I work for John P. Kane, foot of East 14th Street. On the first day of the riot, August 15th, I was with Thomas Hughes. I had been with him to see the Rev. Mr. Williams, in West 54th Street. We returned through 8th Avenue and went through 36th Street. In 36th Street, between 7th and 8th Avenues, we saw a colored man standing. An officer rushed across the street and hit the colored man on the head and felled him to the sidewalk. The colored man was not doing anything. The officer was a heavy man with large red mustache. My friend stopped to assist the man, and the officer ordered him away. Some people from the house close by pulled the colored man in. He was unconscious. I saw a number of colored people struck by officers.

WILLIAM SHEA.

Sworn to before me this 30th day of August, 1900.

FRANK MOSS, Notary Public, N. Y. County.

Statement of Paul Leitenberger and Alfred E. Borman (white), of 105 East 22nd Street:

On August 15th we were on 28th Street, and were going home, walking up 7th Avenue, and at 29th Street a crowd was coming down about ten P. M. We followed the crowd up 35th Street, and it went into the Dorê (a dive), and yelled, "Give us a coon and we'll lynch him!" They then went to Corbett's on Broadway. He has a colored man working for him. Then the police came with their clubs and dispersed the crowd, which went up Broadway. A cable car was coming downtown, and some one cried, "There's a nigger; lynch him!" and several white men jumped on the car. A colored man was standing in the car, and with a cane or umbrella warded off the blows. The car went on with him; the gripman would not stop it, though they called on him to stop. Some of the men were thrown off of the car and nearly run over. There was a Negro on the second car behind that, and the crowd pulled him off, and the man escaped by running into the Marlborough Hotel, where he was sheltered. There were no policemen present at these times, but some policemen appeared and the mob moved up Broadway to about 41st Street, and tried to get into the Vendome Hotel. Some got in, and one cried out, "Give us the coon!" The police coming up, they moved on and went up as far as the Hotel Cadillac at 43rd Street, and went in to get the colored hall man, and an officer came up and clubbed right and left. Other officers came and the crowd scattered. We waited a half hour, and the police kept the people moving. We walked through 42nd Street to 8th Avenue, and saw more of the rioters, and several policemen would not allow them to make any disturbance, and the rioters spread, breaking up. The whole aim of the rioters was to catch Negroes. We saw Devery the first night. We didn't see him the second night. He was in command. We observed the first night that the police generally made no effort to disperse the crowds, but ran along with them. The only places where they attacked the crowds were at Corbett's and the Cadillac. The disturbing element were young fellows, such as frequent "Hell's Kitchen." We talked with a ringleader at the northeast corner of 28th Street and 8th Avenue, a few nights after. He said he had been a leader in the riots and would do it again—that the "niggers" must be treated the same as down South. At the Cadillac there was an officer who did splendid work in dispersing the crowd. For a while he was alone, and he clubbed the crowd indiscriminately; in a little while two other officers came and helped him, and those three men ejected the mob from the hotel, and when they were in the street other officers appeared and effectually dispersed the crowd. This showed what could be done when they wanted to. They protected the hotel in good shape, also Corbett's, when the mob tried to get in.

PAUL LEITENBERGER.
ALFRED E. BORMAN.

Sworn to before me this 13th day of September, 1900.

FRANK MOSS, Notary Public, N. Y. County.

Statement of Frank H. Bertholf (white), 463 West 44th Street:

On the evening of August 16th, 1900, I saw several Negroes kicked and cuffed unnecessarily. Not a white man was touched. All happened in five or ten minutes. Not many Negroes appeared, but when one came in sight he was pounced upon by the crowd, and the policemen made no effort to take care of them, and when they got hold of them they treated them roughly. I saw two Negroes struck by rioters while in the hands of officers, and the officers made no effort to protect them. I saw an officer aim a very vicious blow with his club at a colored man; it seemed it would kill him, but the Negro dodged.

FRANK H. BERTHOLF.

City and County of New York, ss.:

Miss Alice Lee, being duly sworn, deposes and says:

I reside at 433 West 36th Street (in the rear of the 37th Street station house). On the night of Wednesday, August 15th, 1900, also Thursday, the 16th, I heard people screaming and groaning, and shouts of people pleading not to be clubbed any more. I saw one man lying on the station house floor, apparently almost helpless. One man who was pleading seemed to be between the main building and the out building where the cells are located. An officer who was on one of the upper floors leaned out of the window and threw a bottle down at the said man, saying, "Kill the black son of a b———!" Deponent further declared that it was impossible to sleep during both of the aforesaid nights on account of the heartrending shrieks and groans coming from the station house; and further, that she saw a number of colored men lying up in a corner of the station house.

ALICE LEE.

Sworn to before me this 20th day of September, 1900.

GEO. P. HAMMOND, JR., Notary Public (164), N. Y. County.

City and County of New York, ss.:

Cynthia Randolph, being duly sworn, deposes and says:

I reside at 433 West 36th Street, New York City, Manhattan Borough. My home is directly in the rear of the 37th Street station house. On the evening of Wednesday, August 15th, 1900, and the evening of August 16th, 1900, I heard cries and shrieks of people being beaten, coming from the 37th Street station house—such groans as, "O Lord! O Lord! don't hit me! don't hit me!" spoken in pleading tones. This continued all of Wednesday night, with such frequency, and was so heartrending, as to make it impossible to sleep. It was not quite so bad Thursday evening. Deponent states further that it is a common thing to hear coming from the 37th Street station house cries of people, as if they were being beaten, except since last Labor Day; since which day it has been exceptionally quiet.

CYNTHIA RANDOLPH.

Sworn to before me this 15th day of September, 1900.

GEO. P. HAMMOND. JR., Notary Public (164), N. Y. County.

City and County of New York, ss.:

Mrs. Florence Randolph, being duly sworn, deposes and says:

I reside at 117 West 134th Street. On Wednesday, August 15th, 1900, I resided at 433 West 36th Street. On the said 15th of August I was ill in bed, and while I lay in bed I heard at different intervals during the night, and until about three or half past three the next morning, the screams and shouts as of persons in agony, and cries of "Why are you hitting me? I haven't done anything!" Deponent states that these cries and screams came from the 37th Street station house, the rear of which abuts on the rear of the house in which deponent then resided. Deponent states further that her husband was unable to reach his home for four nights on account of the disorder in that neighborhood. Further, that her husband works at 43rd Street and 5th Avenue.

FLORENCE RANDOLPH.

Sworn to before me this 12th day of September, 1900.

GEO. P. HAMMOND, JR., Notary Public (164), N. Y. County.

City and County of New York, ss.:

Susie White, being duly sworn, deposes and says:

I reside at 444 7th Avenue, New York City. On Sunday morning, August 12th, 1900, about six A. M., two officers in full uniform came upstairs and, pushing the door of my room open, said, "Did not a man come up here just now?" I answered, "Yes." The officer then said, "Where is he? Bring him out." I then started to call the man, but before I got to the room the officer had preceded me, and he called the man out (his name is Joe Netherland) and took hold of him, and rubbing his hand over his head said, "Got a scar?" Netherland said, "No. Who are you looking for—the man that cut the officer?" The officer said, "Yes. We're going to make it hot for you niggers!" After making a further examination they found two more men, and after making a close examination of them they found that they were not the men they wanted. After threatening to do up all the "niggers" for killing Officer Thorpe they left.

Susie White.

Sworn to before me this 10th day of September, 1900.

Geo. P. Hammond, Jr., Notary Public (164), N. Y. County.

City and County of New York, ss.:

John Hains, being duly sworn, deposes and says:

I reside at No. 341 West 36th Street. I am a laborer, and am at present employed as a longshoreman at Pier 16, North River. On the evening of August 15th, 1900, I went to bed as usual at 9:30 o'clock. About two o'clock in the morning I was awakened by somebody beating me on the back with a club. When I awoke I found six policemen in the room; they had broken in the door. They asked me for the revolver with which they said I had been shooting out of the window. I told them I did not have a revolver. One of the officers said that he had seen me shoot out of the window. Three officers then began to club me, while the other three were searching the house. They found an old toy revolver, which was broken and not loaded, and could not shoot if it had been loaded, and said that that was the pistol I had used. I denied that, which was the truth. They dragged me out of the house, and proceeded to take me to the station house. I was only in my undershirt, being asleep at the time they broke into the house, and begged them to allow me to put on my trousers and my shoes. They only sneered at this, and one of the officers said, "You'll be d———d lucky if you get there alive." Here another of the officers pulled out a revolver and said, "Let's shoot the d———d nigger," to which a third officer replied, "We can take the black son of a b——— to the station house as he is." When I got to the station house I was bleeding from my head and other parts of my body, as a result of these clubbings. There were only two other persons in our apartments that evening—William Seymour, from whom I rent my apartments, and Walter Gregory. When they saw the officers running into the house, acting as they did, they ran out of the house, leaving me asleep. They did not shoot out of the window, and we never kept any weapons in the house. Mrs. Lucy Jones, who lives next door to us, saw the officers beat me. She was in the house during all this time, and saw no firing from our windows. Her affidavit is hereto annexed. When I arrived at the station house, after the entry had been made on the blotter, I was placed in a cell. Before this I was struck by one of the officers in the station house in front of the sergeant's desk, and in his presence, without any interference on his part. After T was placed in the cell somebody (I believe the police surgeon) bandaged my head. The next morning the police loaned me a pair of old trousers, so that I could be taken to the Police Court. Officer Ohm, one of the officers who struck me and abused me, as aforesaid, made the charge against me; he charged me with firing a pistol through the window. I was brought before the magistrate and he asked me if this was so. I told him it was not, and endeavored to explain matters to him, but he would not listen to me and sent me to the Penitentiary for six months. There were a great many similar cases before him that day, and he was very impatient. I did not have a lawyer to represent me, and I was given no opportunity to deny the false charges of the officer. While I was being taken to the station house one of the officers said to another officer who was clubbing me, "Club as hard as you can; this is a d———d hard head." Another said, "I will teach you d———d niggers to club white people. We will kill half of you." I have the sheet which was on the bed on the night in question. It is full of blood stains. I had six stitches put into my head by a surgeon at the building in which the Magistrates' Court is located on 54th Street. This was before I was taken to Blackwell's Island. After I had been there ten days I was released. I do not know the reason why. Sentenced August 16th, released August 25th, about eight A. M. The only one of the officers I could recognize is Officer Ohm, who made the formal complaint in the Magistrates' Court. I was almost beaten into insensibility that night, and all of the officers were in uniform. Last summer I was employed for the season as a butler by General O. O. Howard, at his summer home in Burlington, Vermont, and I have a recommendation from him. I am not a drinking man, and never was arrested before in my life.

JOHN HAINS.

Sworn to before me this 28th day of August, 1900.

GEO. P. HAMMOND, JR., Notary Public (164), N. Y. County.

City and County of New York, ss.:

Walter Gregory, being duly sworn, deposes and says:

I reside at 107 Prince Street, Brooklyn. On August 15th, 1900, I was boarding with Mr. Seymour at 341 West 36th Street. John Hains, Mr. Seymour, and myself were sitting together at our home until about nine o'clock that evening, when Hains went to bed. Mr. Seymour and I were up until about one o'clock, when we went to bed. In the early part of the evening there was a lot of shouting going on in 36th Street, but I heard no shooting. About two o'clock in the morning we were awakened by shooting in front of the house. Seymour and I walked to the window and looked out to see what was the matter. I did not see any colored people on the street at that time, and the shooting was evidently done by white people. Just then I heard somebody break open the front door of the house. There were several people; they were talking in a noisy manner, but I could not hear what they said. As they reached our door some one rapped on it, and said, "Open the door." I said, "I can't." Mr. Seymour and I hurriedly ran to the fire escape undressed. As we did so we passed Hains, who was fast asleep. I shook him and said, "A big crowd is coming in the house." I do not think he heard what I said, and he fell asleep again. Seymour and I went down the fire escape and into the yard at 339, where we remained until matters had quieted down a little. I could hear Hains say repeatedly, "Don't kill me!" The people in the houses were screaming. About three or four o'clock, when things were quiet again, we went back to our room. The bed in which Hains slept was all bloody. Mrs. Jones, who lived next door, and whose affidavit is hereto annexed, then told me what had happened—precisely the same as in her affidavit hereto annexed. I did not know that the people who broke into the house were policemen. I thought they were the rioters. The pistol found in the apartments was an old broken toy pistol, and could not shoot. We never had a razor or a pistol in the house. While the shooting was going on Hains was fast asleep, and there was no shooting from our windows. I am employed at present on the steamer Shinnecock, of the Montauk Steamboat Company, as second pantryman. I have never been arrested in my life. Since this riot we have not lived at 341 West 36th Street, our home having been broken up by it.

WALTER GREGORY.

Sworn to before me this 6th day of September, 1900.

SAMUEL MARCUS, Notary Public, N. Y. County.

City and County of New York, ss.:

William H. Seymour, of 70 Vanderbilt Avenue, Brooklyn, being duly sworn, deposes and says:

I am employed at Pier 16, E. R. I resided at 341 West 36th Street, New York City, from September, 1899, until August 16th, 1900. At no time during the period above mentioned were there any firearms in the house other than an old broken revolver which was in two pieces, having no cartridges and being entirely useless. Deponent further states that he saw the sheet of bed upon which John Hains was lying and found same to be stained with blood. This was about 4:30 on the morning of August 16th, 1900.

WM. H. SEYMOUR.

Sworn to before me this 6th day of September, 1900.

City and County of New York, ss.:

Lucy A. Jones, being duly sworn, deposes and says:

I reside at 341 West 36th Street, on the fourth floor front, west side. John Hains resides on the same floor on the east side. I have read his affidavit, which is hereto annexed, and so far as it relates to the occurrences at said address on the evening of August 15th it is true. I had only returned to the city at six o'clock that evening, having been in the country for two months. I had been in the house, looking out of the window occasionally. I saw shooting in the street, but this was all done by white people. There were no colored people on the street. This shooting was done mostly by white people living at 342 West 36th Street, which is a tenement, and is occupied by a very low class of rowdies, who have constantly abused and insulted the colored residents of the block. The police officers constantly go in and out of this house. On the night in question I saw a great many police officers enter this house and talk with its occupants. They were shouting and using abusive language, and saying, "Kill every d——d one of the niggers!" "Set the house afire!" etc., etc. About two o'clock in the morning I heard somebody at the door of Mr. Seymour's flat next door, saying, "G— d— you; open this door, or I'll kill every d——d nigger in the house." Mr. Hains, who was the only one in the house just then, was asleep, and he did not open the door. They broke the door open, and I saw them club Hains and accuse him of firing a pistol out of the window. He denied this. Then three of the officers beat him, while the other three were searching the house. They did not find any pistol there, so they came into my apartments, and one of them said to me, "You G— d— black son of a b——, you know a lot about this d——d shooting, and if you don't tell me I'll blow the brains out of you." I told them that they could look through my flat, which they did, but did not find anything. Then they went back to the Seymour flat, and I heard one of the officers say, "I've got the revolver; let's kill the G— d— son of a b——," and began to club him in the head and other parts of his body unmercifully. He begged them to allow him to put on his clothes, but the one who had the revolver said, "Shoot the d——d nigger," and he was led to the station house only in his undershirt. Another officer said, "You will be glad if you get there alive." At one time during this fracas I attempted to look into the Seymour flat to see what was going on, but one of the officers said to me, "You G— d— black b——, get back where you belong, or I'll club the brains out of you." After they left I went into the room, and I found the pillows and sheet on the bed full of blood stains. The people in 342 inspired the policemen, telling them to "Burn the house!" "Lynch the d——d niggers!" etc., etc. I am a widow. My daughter, who is about twenty-one years of age, saw this clubbing, and heard the police use this vile and abusive language. After they had arrested Hains I looked out of my window to see how he was being led by the officers. One of the rowdies in 342 said, "Look at the d——d nigger wench looking out of the window. Shoot her! Shoot her!"

LUCY A. JONES.

Sworn to before me this 28th day of August, 1900.

STEPHEN B. BRAGUE, Notary Public (125), N. Y. County.

City and County of New York, ss.:

Mrs. Louisa Francis, 341 West 36th Street, being duly sworn, deposes and says:

I have been housekeeper of the said 341 West 36th Street for the past eleven years. On Thursday, August 16th, 1900, at two o'clock A. M., I heard a number of pistol shots in the street near my home, and heard shouts of "Go into 341, break in the doors, kill the black sons of b——s"—all the said shouts apparently coming from the direction of 342 across the street. Almost immediately thereafter the doors were broken in, the glass in said doors being smashed, and about seven police officers rushed into the house and commenced shooting and yelling, "Kill the black sons of b——s!" "Put your heads in there, or we'll blow them off!" They went to the fourth floor, where John Hains lived, and dragged him out by the shoulders, his feet dragging, and in that condition he was dragged out into the street. I washed up the blood down from the fourth floor down the staircase to and on each and every landing and including the vestibule. The officers, after staying some time in the house, and ordering Mrs. Freeman, Mrs. Mason, and Mrs. Jones to open their doors, and after searching the same, crossed over the roof to 339 and went through that house.

Mrs. Louisa Francis.

Sworn to before me this 28th day of August, 1900.

Geo. P. Hammond, Jr., Notary Public (164), N. Y. County.

City and County of New York, ss.:

Josephine Bullock, being duly sworn, deposes and says:

I reside at 351 West 36th Street. On Wednesday, August 15th, 1900, about 9:30 o'clock P. M., I saw a crowd chase a colored man and beat him, on the corner of 9th Avenue and 36th Street. The said man succeeded in breaking away from the mob, and ran towards my house. When he reached the stoop some of the male tenants who were seated on the stoop told him to come in there, adding that "if they kill one they might as well kill all of them." All during the evening the rioting continued, and from the rear of the house I heard screams and groans coming from the houses facing on 37th Street. About two o'clock A. M. I heard shooting in the street, and in a short while after I saw two police officers dragging a colored man from 341 West 36th Street, who had on no clothing except a gauze undershirt. The officers were clubbing the colored man, and the man was begging them not to club him, as he had done nothing. The only answer he got was more blows and a reply from one of the officers as follows: "Shut up, you black son of a b———, or I'll kill you." Deponent states further that she got no sleep that night, as the screaming and rioting continued until about half past two or three A. M., when a violent storm came up, and the noise subsided somewhat.

her
Josephine x Bullock.
mark

Sworn to before me this 10th day of September, 1900.

Geo. P. Hammond, Jr., Notary Public (164), N. Y. County.

City and County of New York, ss.:

Mrs. Maggie Zeh, being duly sworn, deposes and says:

I reside at 351 West 36th Street. On Wednesday, August 15th, 1900, I saw a colored man trying to get away from the mob, who were beating him. He tried to get into No. 360, but could not. I then saw the officers who had been standing on the corner of 9th Avenue and 36th Street run towards this man and immediately commenced clubbing him. They clubbed him so unmercifully that the man cried out, "For God's sake kill me and be done with it; don't beat me in this manner," and the last I saw of him they were taking him around into 9th Avenue towards the station house. I also saw a mob coming from 9th Avenue, with about ten or twelve officers in uniform in the lead. The officers were shooting up towards the houses on the north side of the street. Deponent declares that she heard no shooting until the officers came into sight and commenced to shoot at the houses. Deponent further states that between eleven or twelve o'clock she saw a colored man and a woman come from a house on the west side of 9th Avenue. Before this couple reached 9th Avenue she noticed two policemen, who had been standing on the southeast corner of 9th Avenue and 36th Street, enter the saloon on that corner. When the couple had passed the saloon some men who were in citizens' clothes ran into the saloon, and immediately came out again with the aforementioned officers, and pointed to the couple going up the street, and said something to the officers. The officers then followed the said couple up the street to 8th Avenue, where I lost sight of them for about two minutes. At the expiration of that time I looked towards 8th Avenue and I saw the same policemen turning the corner, having in custody the aforementioned couple, and when they reached the front of my house I saw that the man was bleeding and was handcuffed. The woman attempted to speak, when she was ordered with an oath to "shut up." While the officers who were previously mentioned as doing the shooting in 36th Street, the officer who was apparently in command and who wore a cap, and had all the appearance of either a sergeant or a captain, shouted, "Get your heads in out of there if you value your lives." Deponent further states that she has read the affidavit of Josephine Bullock, which affidavit is hereto attached, and she knows of her own knowledge that matters therein stated are true.

MRS. MAGGIE ZEH.

Sworn to before me this 10th day of September, 1900.

GEO. P. HAMMOND, JR., Notary Public (164), N. Y. County.

City and County of New York, ss.:

Richard A. Taylor, being duly sworn, deposes and says:

I reside at 339 West 36th Street; that on Wednesday, August 15th, 1900, I left my home at about 12:15 P. M. to go to my work, as Pullman porter on West Shore R. R.; that when I left my home I left on the shelf in the closet in the front room of my suite between sixty and seventy dollars in bills, which money I was saving to pay my tuition in college next winter; further, my wife did not know that the money was there; that on my return Saturday, August 18th, 1900, between five and six P. M., I was told by my wife of a visit of police officers, about eight in number, each of whom had a revolver in his hand, and who wanted to know if there was a man in the rooms. They were told that there was, and were shown Floyd Wallace, whom they took out with them. They also asked for any firearms, and when told that there were none demanded that a light be made so that they could search. While the light was being brought some of the officers went into the front room and forced open the closet. After they were gone my wife remembered having left her pocketbook in a small satchel on the floor. She immediately ran to the front room, and opening the satchel found that all the money had been taken from her pocketbook except some silver. Deponent on hearing of this immediately went to look for his money and found it gone.

RICHARD A. TAYLOR.

Sworn to before me this 6th day of September, 1900.

GEO. P. HAMMOND, JR., Notary Public (164), N. Y. County.

City and County of New York, ss.:

Mrs. Margaret Taylor, being duly sworn, deposes and says:

I reside at 339 West 36th Street. On Thursday, August 16th, 1900, about two A. M., while lying on a lounge in the front room of my house, I was aroused by hearing a shot fired, followed by several others. I went to the window, when some one in the street shouted with a curse, "Get your head in there or I'll shoot it off." I withdrew my head, and then realized that some of the shots had entered my windows. One imbedded itself in the ceiling, and another passed through a glass door leading into an inner room, and occupied by a lodger named Floyd Wallace. I awoke the said Wallace, and told him that some one was firing into the windows. Shortly after I heard sounds as of a number of people coming down the stairs from the roof, past my door, and stopping on the floor below me. In a very short while they returned, and without asking to be let in broke open my door, and then I saw that they were police officers in full uniform, six in number. They asked me if I knew who fired the shots. I said I did not know. They then told me I lied. Then they asked me if there were any guns in the house, and I answered no; whereupon I was again told that I lied. I then said, "All right, go ahead and search for them," which they proceeded to do. They went from room to room, and broke into a closet in the front room, which contained my husband's and my own clothes; they then opened a small satchel in which was my pocketbook. In the said pocketbook I had six dollars in bills and one dollar and seventy-five cents in silver. While part of the men were making the search the others seized the aforesaid Wallace and took him out into the hallway, where deponent has been told they clubbed the said Wallace on the wrist and face. When he came in, after the officers left, deponent saw that his face and cheek were bruised and his wrist swollen. Deponent declares it to be her belief that the bullets which were shot into her room (one of which she has) could not have been fired from the street, but must have come from the houses opposite. Further, that when the officers left she remembered having left her pocketbook in the aforesaid satchel, and immediately ran into the front room to see if it was safe; she found that the six dollars in bills was gone, and declares it to be her belief that the same was taken by the three officers who were in the room making the search. Deponent further states that when her husband returned on the following Saturday she told him of the visit of the police officers. He then searched in the closet for some money, amounting to about sixty dollars, which he stated to have left there without my knowledge, and could not find it. Deponent declares it to be her belief that this money was also taken by the police officers aforementioned. Deponent further declares that there were no shots fired from her apartments, and that no one therein had a firearm of any sort.

MAGGIE TAYLOR.

Sworn to before me this 7th day of September, 1900.

GEO. P. HAMMOND, JR., Notary Public (164). N. Y. County.

City and County of New York, ss.:

Floyd Wallace, being duly sworn, deposes and says:

I live at 339 West 36th Street. On Thursday, August 16th, 1900, at about 2:30 A. M., I was awakened by Mrs. Taylor, who said that they were shooting in the windows. I immediately arose and dressed, and went into the kitchen. I heard some one screaming, "Don't hit me like that!" and crying as if being beaten. A short while after I heard some one coming over the roof from the house next door (No. 341), and when they reached our door they without any ceremony, and without asking to be let in, broke in the door. I then saw that they were police officers in full uniform. They then asked if there was any man in the house, and was told there was; upon hearing which I stepped to the kitchen door and was immediately seized upon and taken out into the hallway by two of the officers. They started downstairs with me, when one of the officers said, "Wait a minute," and without first telling me to stop they struck me over the arm and on the wrist. The rest of the officers then searched through the rooms, and while they were engaged one of the officers who was with me, without saying a word, jabbed his stick in my face, just missing my eye, and striking me on the cheek bone, under the eye, making a painful bruise. I was perfectly sober, and was sleeping in bed from about 11:30 P. M. till within about five minutes of the time of the visit of the police. I made no resistance, said nothing to them, and showed by my actions a willingness to do as they wished me to. After the officers had finished their search they turned me loose.

FLOYD WALLACE.

Sworn to before me this 7th day of September, 1900.

GEO. P. HAMMOND, JR., Notary Public (164), N. Y. County.

City and County of New York, ss.:

Lloyd Lee, being duly sworn, deposes and says:

I reside at 200 West 37th Street. On Wednesday, August 15th, 1900, about ten o'clock P. M., I was up about West 41st Street near 7th Avenue, when I saw considerable rioting going on, and immediately made an attempt to get to my home, going to 8th Avenue, thence to 38th Street, and thence to 7th Avenue, and had got to within thirty yards of my home when I heard footsteps in the gravel behind me; I turned around and saw a man hatless and in citizen's clothes coming after me; thinking he was a rioter, I jumped aside and asked him what was the matter. He did not answer, but struck me over the head with his club, and when I tried to run away he struck me again. Finding I could not get away, I drew the only weapon I had, namely, a small pocketknife, and cut at him with it. He then drew his revolver, and shot me in the mouth and in the arm. I then run to any front door and slammed it shut, and then opened the inner door, and saw no one around, but I saw a revolver lying on the front steps. I picked it up and took it with me to the roof. After reaching the roof I sank down and knew nothing further until the next day, when I found myself in Bellevue Hospital. I was taken to the 54th Street court and from there remanded to the Tombs, where I remained until September 25th, 1900, when I was brought to Part I, where I was discharged.

LLOYD LEE.

Sworn to before me this 1st day of October, 1900.

GEO. P. HAMMOND, JR., Notary Public (164), N. Y. County.

(The Grand Jury refused to indict Lloyd Lee.)

City and County of New York, ss.:

Mrs. Nettie Threewitts, being duly sworn, deposes and says that she resides at No. 200 West 37th Street; that on Wednesday, August 15th, 1900, about half past ten, she was preparing to retire, when her stepfather, Lloyd Lee, came to her door, and she asked him what was the matter. He replied, "Nettie, I'm shot!" He then ran to the roof. Almost immediately after she heard two men come into the hallway, and one said, "Get your revolver out!" They then came up to the hallway where I was standing, and I saw that one was an officer in uniform and one in citizen's clothes, a stout man. I asked them, "What's the matter?" They said, "Where's that man?" I answered, "I don't know." They then said, "Who is the man?" I answered, "He's my stepfather." The man in citizen's clothes then said, "She's got blood on her; take her; she's a prisoner." I then said, "You are not going to take me without any clothes on?" He answered, "You don't need any clothes." I was then brought downstairs and kept on the stoop until the patrol wagon came, where a number of officers who were standing there called me a "black b——," and one of them struck me in the head with his fist, another one deliberately spit in my face, and another took his helmet and jabbed it into my eye. This officer's number was either No. 3062 or 3064. The latter occurred while I was on my way to the West 54th Street police court. Among the other remarks which were made to me was, "They ought to burn up all the nigger ranches;" "Shut up, you're a w——, the same as the rest of them." I was kept in the station house without any additional clothes for about two hours, when a woman who lives on 41st Street gave me an underskirt, which I put on. I was then brought into the room back of the main room, and from there was taken back into a cell. I was arraigned in the 54th Street police court and held in $500 bail for trial. Mr. R. T. Varnum went on my bond.

NETTIE THREEWITTS.

Sworn to before me this 19th day of September, 1900.

GEO. P. HAMMOND, JR., Notary Public (164), N. Y. County.

City and County of New York, ss.:

William Devan, being duly sworn, deposes and says:

I reside at 403 West 29th Street. On Wednesday, August 15th, 1900, about half past ten, while walking on 8th Avenue, between 28th and 29th Streets, I was attacked by a mob and shoved through a glass show case, cutting my head severely. I managed to get away from the mob and run towards 8th Avenue and 28th Street, where I was stopped by a policeman, who grabbed me, and the mob coming up at that moment some of them shouted, "Arrest him; he has just broken a show case." I replied that I did not, but that I had been shoved through it. The officer said, "Shut up, or I'll shove this stick down your throat." He then took me to the station house in West 37th Street, where I was detained from 10:30 P. M. till four A. M. the next day. While in the station house I saw a man brought in who had nothing on but an undershirt, and who was bleeding from wounds in his head. I also saw Lee brought in, and saw the surgeon administer an injection, and put him into the ambulance, saying, "This fellow is almost gone," and rushed him off to the hospital. I also saw Miss Lee, the aforementioned man's daughter, who was brought to the station house with nothing but her nightgown on, and one of the women in the station house loaned her a dress to put on.

WILLIAM DEVAN.

Sworn to before me this 11th day of September, 1900.

GEO. P. HAMMOND, JR., Notary Public (164), N. Y. County.

City and County of New York, ss.:

William Hopson, being duly sworn, deposes and says:

I reside at 229 West 60th Street. I am engaged in the jewelry business, and am night engineer at the Scarborough Apartment House, 221 West 57th Street. On Sunday, August 26th, 1900, in the afternoon, I was standing a little way from my door, about ten yards, and saw Officer 4600 walking on 60th Street from 10th to 11th Avenue. After he passed me he met a platoon of policemen who were coming from 11th Avenue towards 10th Avenue, and turned back with them. Opposite 225 West 60th Street there were two colored men sitting in front of the door. Officer 4600 came over and without warning struck one of them. As he did so the other one ran into the house. The man he was beating also attempted to run in, but he ran after him striking him on the head with his fist. (This was James A. Scott, 225 West 60th Street.) He then came over to me, struck me on the side of the head, and said, "What are you doing here?" I said, "I am looking on," and attempted to go into my apartments. He followed me and struck me with his clenched hand on my head. This was within five feet of my door. Here he was joined by two other officers, one of whom struck me a blow with his club, full force on the head and eye, and I was unable to see anything with that eye for some time after; it is bloodshot still. I held on to the iron railing in front of 231, to protect myself in that way if I could. As I did so two more officers came. Three of them were clubbing me, and 4600 was striking me with his fist. The officer who struck me in the eye with his club was about 6 feet 2 inches tall. They tore my coat and broke my hat. Some one attempted to hand me my hat as they knocked it off, but one of the officers knocked it out of the person's hand with his club, and said, "Never mind the hat." This was as I was being led to the station house. When we reached No. 227 Officer 4600, who had me in charge, saw Mr. Myers, the janitor of 227, standing in front of the door with his wife and several other persons. Mr. Myers is a colored man. Officer 4600 turned me over to another officer and said, "Take my prisoner to the station house." The officer replied, "No, don't take him there." 4600 insisted, and the officer obeyed. When Officer 4600 went over to Myers he wanted to strike him. Myers is a sick man and just got out of the hospital. His wife pleaded with the officer not to strike him, whereupon the officer turned Myers loose and raised his club to strike his wife. One of the other officers told 4600 not to strike that woman. Then five or six officers jumped on Myers with their clubs. There were about ten policemen altogether. 4600 struck him with his fist. One officer broke his club into pieces on Myers' head. Myers was taken to Roosevelt Hospital. He told me in court the next day that as he was passing 60th Street and 10th Avenue they saw a colored man having his shoes shined. 4600 said to him, "See that black nigger? If I didn't have you I would drag him out and lay his head open the same as yours." Myers told me that the doctor at the hospital recognized him and asked him what was the matter. The officer told Myers to "shut up," and said to the doctor, "That is my prisoner." I was taken to the station house, where the officer who brought me there made the complaint against me for Officer 4600. He told the sergeant I "showed fight." I was not told what the formal charge against me was. The sergeant asked me nothing but the usual questions, what my name was, etc. I was bleeding from my eye. The colored people and the whites on this street have always been very friendly, and are so even now. There never was any trouble until these officers raised the disturbance on that day. Officer 4600 started the thing. Some of the tenants of Nos. 227, 229, and 231 saw this outrageous treatment on the part of the policemen. We were discharged in court the next day, after 4600 had made his complaint to the magistrate. I have been in New York for over eight years, and have never been arrested before in my life. I was employed in Harris & Flippin's sporting goods store in Richmond, Va., for two years; I was employed by Oscar Miller, 154 Chambers Street, coffee and spice dealer, for ten months at his residence in Sing Sing; I was employed by C. E. Vedder, druggist, at 116th Street and Madison Avenue, for three years; I was employed by Andrew Lester, of 56th Street and 8th Avenue, at the Washington Apartments, for ten months; I was employed by the Goldsoll Diamond Palace, 14th Street, about two years; W. P. Unger, dealer in essence oils, 18 Cedar Street, for ten months; Van Boskerck & Wilson, 132 West 21st Street, dressmakers, for ten months. I am now employed by Mr. Condit, of the firm of Acker, Merrill & Condit, at the Scarborough Apartment House, 221 West 57th Street. I have been so employed for about two years. I did nothing which justified my arrest or this action on the part of the police.

WILLIAM HOPSON.

Sworn to before me this 31st day of August, 1900.

GEO. P. HAMMOND. JR., Notary Public (164), N. Y. County.

City and County of New York, ss.:

George L. Myers, being duly sworn, deposes and says that he resides at 227 West 60th Street, Manhattan Borough, New York City; that on Sunday, August 26th, 1900, at about half past one, he went downstairs, hearing a noise, and being janitor of No. 225 as well as 227, naturally he wanted to see everything was all right on the premises. He was standing in the doorway of No. 227 when the officers approached and said to him, "What are you doing here?" He answered, "Nothing." One of the officers then said, "I'll place you under arrest." "All right," he answered, "take me along." The said officer then struck him with his fist under the left jaw, and then grabbed him and struck him over the head with his club, knocking him insensible. When he recovered consciousness he was on the corner of Amsterdam Avenue and 60th Street, and in charge of Officer John J. Cleary, who took him to the Roosevelt Hospital. While on the way there said Officer Cleary continued to strike deponent with his clinched fist, saying, "There's one for luck," and "If I had got you first I would not have struck you with my fist. I would have used my club on your head and killed you." Deponent was taken to the station house, where he was charged with "interfering with an officer in the discharge of his duty," and "attempting to rescue a prisoner." The same charge was made the next morning in the Police Court, where he was discharged. Deponent declares that he was perfectly sober, and was downstairs by reason of his being janitor of the aforementioned houses, and it was his duty to be where he was and at that time; that he has never been arrested in his life before, and that he did not attempt to rescue anyone from the custody of an officer, and that the assault was entirely unjustified and an outrage.

GEO. L. MYERS.

Sworn to before me this 5th day of September, 1900.

GEO. P. HAMMOND, JR., Notary Public (164), N. Y. County.

City and County of New York, ss.:

Mrs. Frances C. Myers, being duly sworn, deposes and says that she is the wife of George L. Myers, and that she resides at 227 West 60th Street; that she has read the affidavit of the said George L. Myers, her husband, and that she knows the facts therein stated to be true of her own knowledge and belief. Deponent further states that while her husband was being clubbed she implored and begged the officers not to strike her husband, as he was a cripple, and had done nothing, but they continued to strike him, and one of the officers drew off as if to strike her with his fist, and another as if to strike her with his billy, but she got out of their way, and when she saw an officer break his billy over her husband's head she thought they had killed him, and she then went on upstairs. The officers refused to even allow her to pick up his hat.

FRANCES C. MYERS.

Sworn to before me this 5th day of September, 1900.

GEO. P. HAMMOND, JR., Notary Public (164), N. Y. County.

City and County of New York, ss.:

James A. Scott, being duly sworn, deposes and says:

I reside at 225 West 60th Street. On Sunday afternoon, August 26th, some officers went down the street towards 11th Avenue. They were pursuing bad boys who had made a disturbance in the morning. I saw them from my window, and after they reached 11th Avenue I went down to the door, and stood there looking towards 11th Avenue, where there was a crowd. There were only two persons near me, nearly all of the persons who were on the street having gone down to the avenue; one was a boy named Smith, and another young man who has moved away. An officer whom I have since learned is John J. Cleary, came from 10th Avenue towards me. He spoke to me before I saw him, saying, "Do you live here?" and I turned to see who spoke to me, and as I turned towards him, before I could reply he struck me a hard blow on my head with a hard substance, which dazed me, and he followed it with a blow of his fist in the mouth, and I went down in a heap. I began to bleed profusely from the mouth. I was in my doorway when he struck me, so that I fell into my hall. He did not attempt to arrest me. I went upstairs, and I heard a woman's voice screaming, "Don't beat my husband." I looked out of the window and saw the same policeman, Cleary, and other officers whom I cannot identify, clubbing George L. Myers. The principal clubber was the said Cleary. I saw him club the said Myers on the head until he broke his club, and saw him pulling Myers up 60th Street, and punching him with his fist. Myers was dreadfully beaten and was bleeding badly.

JAMES A. SCOTT.

Sworn to before me this 24th day of September, 1900.

FRANK MOSS, Notary Public, N. Y. County.

(The case of Hopson, Myers, and Scott is substantiated by fully twenty witnesses.)

City and County of New York, ss.:

John Wolf, of No. 347 West 37th Street, being duly sworn, deposes and says:

On Sunday, September 30, I was visiting a female friend, and two officers came in with a woman I had known, and who claimed to be my wife but was not. The officers ordered me to leave the house, and I did so. I asked the officers, "Why?" and one of them said, "If I catch you here again I will lock you up." I never had any experience in court or in such matters before, and I went to the station house for advice. I went to the sergeant at the desk, and told him that I was in trouble, and without experience, and I wanted to be advised. He said, "What is the matter with you?" I said, "Can a woman that I have lived with have me arrested because I don't want to live with her any more?" He answered, "What are you talking about? You get out of here!" I was surprised, and didn't move quickly enough to suit him, and he ordered an officer to arrest me. The officer stepped up to me in front of the desk, pulled a billy from his pocket, and suddenly struck me a hard blow on my right jaw, which broke it and caused my chin to fall down. The officer hurried me back to a cell. I suffered terrible agony and walked up and down my cell all night calling for relief. I paid thirty-five cents to send out a message to Mr. Young, who was not at home. His son came, but was not allowed to see me. I had no attention at all, and in the morning was arraigned in court. The officer was on the bridge close to the judge; I was down on the floor. I couldn't hear what charge he made or what he said. My face was swelled and mouth almost closed, and I could not make any statement. The justice fined me three dollars on the officer's statement, and the police attendants hustled me along. I had no money to pay my fine, and was sent back to the court prison. I was in an awful condition. I lay down on some boards, but couldn't stay still. I moaned, and cried for help, but could not get anyone to notice my case. The night man who came on duty on Monday night was a humane man, and asked what was my trouble, and I told him as well as I could. He rang for an ambulance, and I was taken to Bellevue Hospital. I reached there 9:30 P. M., Monday, and was put to bed, and remained there till four P. M., Wednesday. I was unable to take nourishment while there. When I was discharged I went to the station house for my personal effects, and the officer then in charge asked me my trouble (for my head was swathed in bandages), and I told him, and he caused me to remain and identify the officer who hit me. He scolded the officer, who answered nothing, and he sent me to Police Headquarters to Inspector Thompson with a note, and ever since that time they have been investigating my case, and I have gone back and forth a good many times. Inspector Thompson, in my hearing, complained bitterly of the ruffianly conduct of the officers in the 20th Precinct. He told of a case where one had beaten a colored woman eighty-one years of age, and was afterwards found helplessly drunk in a saloon; he said they were bringing disgrace on the police force. He seemed to try to get the evidence in my case all right, but the trouble is that six policemen and the sergeant swore that they were in the room when I was arrested and that they did not see any blow struck, but they could not account for my broken jaw. This perjury was awful. I am feeling very badly—have just now come from the hospital. I go there every day for treatment. My jaw is still loose, and will not hold in position without the bandages that almost cover my face and head. The doctor at the hospital says that the blow must have been a very hard one, for the bone is crushed. I am poor, and cannot work now. I suffered also in the riot on the 15th of August. I was going to my home, which was then at 245 West 32nd Street, and was pulled off an 8th Avenue car by the mob, and was pelted with stones and beaten with sticks. At first the police who were near by did not interfere, but after I was severely hurt they came over, and as I was down on my hands and knees, trying to get up, one of the officers struck me three blows on my body with his club, and ordered me to get up and get out. I was then quite near my home, and I ran over there, and was pulled in by my friends. The mob and the police chased me. The police hurt me more than the rioters. I had a friend with me, and the police clubbed him also. He ran into my house with me, and stayed there. When the policemen ordered me to get out I was surrounded by the mob that was beating me, and they made no effort to interfere with them. I have always been a hard-working man, and was never before arrested.

JOHN WOLF.

Sworn to before me this 11th day of October, 1900.

FRANK MOSS, Notary Public, N. Y. County.

City and County of New York, ss.:

William J. Elliott, being duly sworn, says:

My name is William J. Elliott. I reside at 209 East 59th Street. At the time of the riot, on August 15th, I lived at 327 West 35th Street. I moved from that side of the town right at once on account of the riot. I am twenty-six years of age and weigh about 130 pounds, and am employed at the Hotel Imperial. I have been there nearly two years. I finished my grammar school education in 1887. I entered the Florida State Normal College in 1894; I was there for two sessions, from '94 to '95. I left there and entered into a drug firm by the name of Martinez & Co., Jacksonville, Florida, as an apprentice to study pharmacy, and in less than a year my advancement was so good I was made a prescriptionist. I then came to New York and entered a drug firm by the name of C. K. Harris Beach Pharmacy at Atlantic City, N. J. I was a trustworthy man there, generally useful; during one fall had entire charge of one of two of Mr. Harris' drug stores in Atlantic City. Mr. Harris sold out, and after that I sought other work, and I came here to New York City. My intention has been to accumulate enough money to take a pharmaceutical course. On the night of August 14th there came a colored man to the Hotel Imperial and informed the front door man that there were riots in the street and that there was no way of getting home. This was between nine and ten o'clock in the evening. About 12:15 I was off duty, and left the hotel with John Chism, the front door man; we went out to investigate and see if the boys could get home. We had no sooner got to 6th Avenue and 31st Street than a fierce mob came chasing down the street and in hot pursuit of a colored man, yelling, "Kill the nigger! Lynch him!" We then ran towards Broadway, and were met there by Mr. Murphy, a man who keeps a saloon at 31st Street and 6th Avenue. He advised us to go at once back to the hotel and to tell the chief, Mr. Roberts, to keep all of his men in the hotel that night or they would get killed. We went back, and I delivered the message to Chief Roberts, and he advised and told all the men to stay in. Chism, Travers, and myself came out to the front door again, and saw a Negro running for his life by the Hotel Imperial through 32nd Street towards 5th Avenue, with a mad crowd behind him. Then we were made to come into the hotel by the chief, as the hotel people were afraid that the mob might attack the house. I remained in the hotel all night. Mr. Chism and I tried to get a closed cab to drive three of us home, but the cabman said he would not drive us home for $500. This was the night of the riot in which so many were injured. At five o'clock the next morning I left the Hotel Imperial to go home with Leon Vonce. I walked as far as 36th Street and 8th Avenue with him, as I intended to go to his home with him, as he was very anxious about his wife; he was afraid she might have been attacked. When we got to the corner of 36th Street and 8th Avenue I saw a big white man jump on one of two colored boys, whom I know to be hotel boys going to their work. I got a little uneasy at the sights I saw, and I saw some blood on the sidewalk, and Leon Vonce said to me, "You had better turn around and go home," and I did, and went to bed. At half past eleven I awoke and dressed myself and got out of the house by a quarter to twelve noon, and got as far as Rocky's drug store, corner 34th Street and 8th Avenue. A white boy standing on the corner said to me, "You had better go away from around here, or you will get killed." I then noticed groups of boys and men running from 34th Street down 8th Avenue; they were right across the street from me, and at sight of them I became afraid that they would attack me and I ran home. I had, however, to get to my work, as I knew the hotel people needed me, and I was afraid that some of the other men would not be able to get back to the hotel; so after a little while I made another attempt to go to the hotel. I went out of the house. I was then addressed by a white man, who seemed to be much of a gentleman. He says (this was when I reached 8th Avenue), "For God's sake, boy, you had better go away from here. Go ahead, jump on that car; they just near killed a colored man across the street." Then as he said that I heard the crowd yell, "There's a nigger! there's a nigger! Catch him!" Luckily for me, I jumped on a car and there was a colored boy on the corner by Comford Brothers' saloon. The mob saw him and ran after him; they caught the colored boy and the mob grabbed and gathered around him. They were rough-looking fellows, and I could not see what they did to the colored boy, for he was in the center of this mob. The car I jumped on was a green car and went across 9th Avenue on 34th Street. I jumped off at 9th Avenue, and just as I left the car there were four big white fellows said, "There's a d——d nigger!" and they started at me, and I ran home as hard as I could, and when I reached home I was all out of breath. When I got home the folks at home asked me if I had anything to protect myself. I told them no, I had nothing; I never had any use for such things. There was a colored gentleman stopping there, Mr. Miles. He said it was very dangerous for me to go out, but if I intended going out at all he had a little gun upstairs, which probably would be some protection from the mob. I thanked him very much, and took the gun, a little .22 caliber revolver. I still felt it necessary for me to go back to the hotel, and I thought I would get back by going another way, and for an hour and a half I stood on my stoop and in the house at times waiting for an opportunity to get by the crowd on 8th Avenue and elsewhere; this was about half past two or quarter to three in the afternoon. I started and went west towards 9th Avenue, thinking I could take a car going north to 42nd Street, and then across 42nd Street and down Broadway to the Hotel Imperial at 32nd Street and Broadway. Just as I got to 35th Street and turned the corner on 9th Avenue there was a mob of three or four hundred men and boys just below me coming up 9th Avenue, screaming and hollering and following a car and yelling, "Take the nigger off the car!" "Catch the nigger!" and "Kill the nigger!" and I turned then and I ran up 9th Avenue as hard as I could from the mob, and I ran into a pawnbroker's shop, Mr. Weaver's pawnshop. I stood behind the closed doors, and through the small openings or blinds that the pawnbrokers have over their doors I could see that part of the big crowd that stood in front of the pawnbroker's shop, many of whom were lined up on the sidewalk across the street. I could also see a policeman trying to disperse the men with his club. He was hitting with his club right and left to clear the sidewalk. I saw three guns hanging in the pawnbroker's window, and I said to the pawnbroker, "Let me see those guns there." I had not any intention of buying the guns, and did not buy them, but I thought it would be a bluff to make the crowd think I had something. I told the pawnbroker's clerk I did not want a gun at that time, I would come back. While I was pricing the guns a great big white fellow opened the door, put his head in, and looked suspiciously around the room. He gave me one of those staring looks, and then shut the door. Then Mr. Weaver, the owner of the pawnshop, said, "Don't you go out there; they are waiting out there for you; they will beat you." After staying there for over half an hour, listening to the hollering outside of "Kill the nigger!" "Lynch the nigger!" and the crowd running about the street chasing other negroes, a great many of whom lived in that locality, I asked the clerk if I could go upstairs and hide, as I was afraid they might come in after me; but he said, "No one dasen't come in here." Shortly after this conversation I asked this clerk if it was safe to go out. He said yes, the crowd was chased down the Avenue. I also asked Mr. Weaver if it was safe to go out now. He said he thought everything was over now. I went to the door and peeped out, and I only saw a few people in groups and four boys standing right at the pawnbroker's door a little to the left of me. I called to one of these white boys, and asked him if it was safe for me to go out. He asked me where did I want to go. I told his as far as 42nd Street. He said, "Go to one of those cops and he will take you up." I saw some cops at 36th Street corner. I started toward the cops to ask them to take me up to 42nd Street, but I had not gone half a dozen steps towards where the cops were when a man in citizen's clothes grabbed me. I learned afterwards he was an officer, and he asked me where I was going. I told him I was trying to get to my work. He asked me what I was doing in a pawnbroker's shop. Before I could explain he said I had bought a gun, and commenced to search me. At that time there were four policemen around me. The little .22 caliber gun he found and took from my pocket. I offered no resistance, and only asked him for protection from the mob, which commenced to gather again, and were now yelling, "Kill the nigger!" "Lynch the nigger!" This mob came up close behind me with sticks and stones. One of the officers knocked on the sidewalk with his club, and there were about half a dozen more officers ran to us to keep the mob off me. The mob was kept off me, and the officer in citizen's clothes and a policeman in uniform took hold of each of my shoulders and four policemen followed behind me. The mob went along too, yelling and screaming, "Kill the nigger!" "Lynch the nigger!" We went west on 37th Street towards the 37th Street station, which is between 9th and 10th Avenues, when we turned into 37th Street. Then the two officers in charge of me and two more behind me took me to the 37th Street station house. Up to this time I had not received a blow, and was not injured in any way. They stood me before a man who sat behind a desk in the station house. There were lots of people there. Some of the men were in citizens' clothes. The man behind the desk said to the officer who had me in charge, "What is the charge against this man?" and the officer in citizen's clothes said, "Carrying a concealed weapon he bought out of a pawnshop." I said, "I did not buy any weapon there," and the man behind the desk said, "Don't dictate to us about what you did not do," and then I started to tell him about my reputation and not being a rioter, and that I was only trying to get to my work. He said, "We have got no time to look up your reputation. Lock him up." I was taken by the jailer who is in the station house, and he said, "Come on," and took hold of me. There were two doors leading from the office into the muster room, and I went to get through the left-hand door. Right beside the door in the station house was a policeman leaning against the door. As I passed him he threw out his foot and tripped me. I stumbled but did not fall. I did not see the jailer; he let go of my coat he had hold of. I looked around at the man who tripped me. As I looked around another policeman struck me on the jaw with his fist; then another struck me in the back of the head with his club, and all the policemen in the muster room jumped up and jumped on me, yelling, "Kill him!" "Kill the nigger!" I still stood up and received many punches. I begged for mercy, and did not weaken until an officer struck me in the temple with his billy, and everything was dark around me. I fell down, and I could still feel them kicking and beating me about. This time the man behind the desk, who I believe is Captain Cooney, rushed in and said, "Don't kill that man in here. The reporters are out here, and there is going to be a charge made against you, and if another man touches a prisoner in here I will take a hand in it myself;" and he says, "Lock that man up." At that time I held my hands above my head and was running around trying to find the doorway to the cells. I was then taken and locked up. I am still sick and ill from the blows that I received, and my right eye is affected. It quivers and is bloodshot, and the right part of my head and temple is sore. I stayed in the police station all night, and sent a telegram to the hotel people at the Imperial, and the manager sent a detective over to get me out, but the detective was afraid to take me out. The next morning I was arraigned before Magistrate Cornell for carrying a concealed weapon. Magistrate Cornell picked up the pistol and said, "Is this your gun?" and laughed, and said that a man with a bad reputation would carry no such gun as that; but he said, "We will have to charge you three dollars for carrying a concealed weapon." I paid the fine and went straight to Travers' house, where my head was bathed in hot water and alcohol, and he rubbed my side and back. I remained there in bed all day. I was unable to work for two days, and then I went back. Since I went back Captain Cooney has sent for me twice, but I have been afraid to go back there. I can bring more evidence to show that after I came out of the police station my head was swollen half its size again, and I could hardly open my mouth, and for two days I had difficulty in eating. I cannot open my mouth right wide now.

WILLIAM J. ELLIOTT.

Sworn to before me this 24th day of August, 1900.

HERBERT PARSONS, Notary Public, N. Y. County.

(On the hearing before Commissioner York three newspaper reporters corroborated Elliott, but a host of policemen contradicted him. Elliott and his witnesses were badgered by Mr. York, and the policemen were led and protected. Counsel was not permitted to take part.)

City and County of New York, ss.:

My name is Harry Reed. I reside at 346 West 41st Street, in the Borough of Manhattan, City of New York. On August 15th, 1900, I was over in Brooklyn and was coming home with four companions. About half-past twelve I reached the corner of 34th Street and 8th Avenue. We five boys were sitting on the seat of an open 8th Avenue car. When we got at the corner of 37th Street and 8th Avenue we saw a mob, and the mob called out, "There's some niggers; lynch them!" and they made a rush for the car, and I jumped out. Then I ran up to the corner of 38th Street, where there were four policemen. Of these four policemen three were standing on the corner, and one ran into the street to stop me. When he saw me coming I was running hard, fast as I could. When I reached this policeman in the street, he hit me over the head with his club. He hit me twice over the head, and I saw the other three policemen coming, and I fell down. I thought if I fell down the others would not attack me, but they did; they hit me over the legs and on my arm, when I raised it up to protect my head, and they hit me in the back. The two cops started to take me to the police station, but when they saw a patrol wagon come around the corner of 38th Street into 8th Avenue they called the patrol wagon, and both went with me in the patrol wagon to the station house, where I stayed till about four o'clock in the morning. There was no charge made against me in the station house. After my head was bound up, and at about four o'clock in the morning, a man dressed in citizen's clothes said, "Two at a time can go when they want to; things are quieted down somewhat." I asked him if anybody was going with us, and they said, "No, go by yourself." I went directly home, where I stayed and went to bed. I got up at about half-past eight and went to the Roosevelt Hospital the next morning. They told me at the station house to go to the hospital. I have been up to the Roosevelt Hospital three times, on the 16th, 17th, and 18th. I don't think I will go any more, but still I have to wear a bandage and dress my head. The scar that I have got on my head is about two inches long, and I was also hit and a bump was raised on the back of my head, but the skin is not broken. I bled a great deal from the wound on my head; my shirt, collar, and tie were all blood-spotted. I am about fifteen years old; one of my companions, who is about twenty-four years old, was knocked down, kicked in the face, and thrown down a cellar by a mob. He is my father's son-in-law; his name is Joe Walker, and he resides at 346 West 41st Street. My other companions did not get hurt at all. One of them started to jump from the car, but a policeman told him to get back, and he stayed on the car, and the mob left him there because they were chasing me and the other fellow. This man was about nineteen or twenty years old. Of my other companions, one was a white boy about nineteen years old, and the mob did not touch him, and he stayed on the car. The other colored boy, who is about fifteen years old, is light-complexioned in color, and the mob did not touch him; he stayed on the cars also. We were in the third seat from the front; we were all sitting on the same seat. I was on the right hand and outside coming up, and when I saw the mob coming along the street from the right I clambered past the other fellows and jumped over the rail on the left, and was the first fellow out. I ran uptown towards 38th Street, where I saw these cops. I wanted to get protection, but instead the cops hit me, as I have told. I did not resist arrest, and I did not struggle to get away from the cops. I only wanted to get away from the mob. The cops stopped me, and did not catch hold of me until I had got down and the other cop had hit me, and one of them caught hold of me to make me stand up. I did not even try to run away after I had been hit. I was afraid to run, because I knew if I did they would hit me again.

Harry Reed.

Sworn to before me this 22nd day of August, 1900.

John C. Barr, Notary Public, Kings County. Certificate filed in N. Y. County.

City and County of New York, ss.:

My name is Jesse Payne. I reside at 255 West 93rd Street. I work there as a waiter in a boarding house. On the evening of August 15th I was sent down to accompany a small boy, by the name of Allan Atkins, to his home, 223 West 18th Street. He took an 8th Avenue car at 93rd Street, and I rode alongside the car until I got to 59th Street. I told him I would ride on, and I rode about a block in front of the car. We went down this way until we approached 34th Street. Around the corner of 34th Street and 8th Avenue I saw a crowd standing. It stretched all over the street and sidewalk. I thought that some one was hurt, and that was the reason the crowd had collected, but when I got into the crowd they did not seem to be standing around no one, and I did not know what was the matter until I passed 34th Street, and was about half way to 33rd Street. I was still on the west side of the car track riding on the wheel, and about half a block in front of the car in which the boy was, and about half a block behind another car, trying to follow the pathway it made in the street. When I got to the middle of the block a policeman ran out from the sidewalk from the west and raised his club and hit me across the mouth, saying, "What the hell are you riding here for?" This blow split my lip and broke off two of my front teeth; it also knocked me off the wheel, but I scrambled up and ran between the east side of 8th Avenue, dragging my wheel with me, and away from the policeman. The policeman followed right upon me, clubbing me, and the whole crowd was after me. I tried to get into a store, and they shoved me back, and they would not let me in. While I was going from where I was knocked off my wheel to the east side of the street a policeman who struck me kept on clubbing me. The first blow he gave me knocked me kind of foolish, but I hung on to my wheel. When I got to the curb I fell, because I missed the step. After I got up another policeman came up to me and said, "What the hell are you doing here with that wheel?" I says, "I ain't done nothing to anybody, just going on a message to take a boy home;" and he grabbed the wheel and hit me over the hand with his club. That made me let go the wheel. It was taken away from me and I have not seen it since. Then I ran away about four doors from 8th Avenue, and a third officer told me to stop and sit down, "If you don't they will kill you;" and he stood there and protected me until he sent another officer for a patrol wagon and took me to the station house, and I was there until four o'clock in the morning. I have been employed by Mrs. McFarland, at 255 West 93rd Street for about three months; before that with Annie Sterler, of 44 West 35th Street—this is a boarding house, and I was a waiter there for two years; with Mrs. Gillies, of 18 West 9th Street, two and a half years. I know Rev. Mr. Franklin, of Zion Church, corner 10th and Bleecker Streets.

his
JESSE x PAYNE.
mark

Sworn to before me this 22nd day of August, 1900.

SAMUEL L. WOLFF, Notary Public (77), N. Y. County.

City and County of New York, ss.:

My name is John B. Mallory. I reside at 206 West 62nd Street. While coming home from the engineers' lectures my friend Gordon Jones and myself came up to 7th Avenue through 29th Street where the colored Engineers' Hall is. We turned into 39th Street and went west towards 8th Avenue. We saw a crowd of white men and boys coming around the corner towards us. Before the gang reached us a policeman said to my friend and myself, "Get out of here," and began clubbing me and my friend; he struck my friend first, and my friend ran towards Broadway. Then after being struck four or five times, and as soon as I could, I ran up on a stoop. The policeman did not have a hold of me, but began striking me, and kept up with me. When I got on top of the stoop he ran after me, and caught hold of me and shoved me down. He said again, "Get out of here." It made me fall down the stairs, and I was on my hands and knees on the walk. Then the policeman left me at the mercy of the mob, and he went across the street where he was at first. The mob began punching me, hitting me with sticks, kicking and hitting me with their fists, and split my lip open, cut my nose, and bruised my forehead. Then I got up and put my hands on my face and head, and stood up against the railing by the stoop of the house where I was shoved down. Then another policeman came to me and said to me, "Have you sense enough to go home?" I said "Yes." I got on an 8th Avenue car, in which he got on, and began going uptown about fifteen or twenty feet, when another policeman came up and got on the car from the left-hand side, and shoved me out towards the right-hand side, where the mob was. He said, "Get out of here." As I was pushed off a man at the side struck at me, but I dodged him and jumped on the car again. The car was moving when the policeman shoved me off of it. The policeman who protected me made the motorman stop the car for me to get on, and I got on the front of the car again. The policeman who protected me said to the policeman who shoved me off, "Get off, and let him alone." He got off then. The policeman who protected me stood on the car until I got up one block out of the mob, and then he got off. I rode on this 8th Avenue car up to 59th Street, and I stood between two men. One of them offered me his handkerchief to wipe the blood off my face, and when I got to 59th Street they advised me to go to Roosevelt Hospital, and I asked one of them to get a transfer for me. He did this, and I went to Roosevelt Hospital, where I had three stitches put in my lip. I am still going to the hospital, and am under treatment; my back and both shoulders are injured, and I am generally bruised all over. I have no bad habits. I do not smoke or drink, and I am a student at the International Correspondence School, Scranton, Pa. I have been through the public schools, and I am studying to be a mechanical engineer. I also attend lectures at the Colored Engineers' Association, on 29th Street between 6th and 7th Avenues. I know Mrs. S. E. Lodewick, of 800 Lexington Avenue; C. W. Phillips, 11 Broadway; L. P. Sawyer, Mrs. J. F. Aitken, Mrs. Mary Baker, Mrs. E. R. Clark, and Mrs. A. Arnold, all of 153 Madison Avenue. I have known these people for about eight years, and they can all testify to my good character.

JOHN B. MALLORY.

Sworn to before me this 22nd day of August, 1900.

SAMUEL L. WOLFF, Notary Public (77), N. Y. County.

City and County of New York, ss.:

Nicholas J. Sherman, being duly sworn, deposes and says:

My name is Nicholas J. Sherman. I reside at No. 134 West 33rd Street, Borough of Manhattan, City of New York. On the 15th day of August I was visiting some friends at 37th Street near 7th Avenue, in a boarding house. As the clock struck ten I left the house. I walked east toward 7th Avenue. At the corner of 37th Street and 7th Avenue I saw several policemen chasing a person eastward. I do not know whether the person was colored or not. I am a messenger and mailing clerk on the New York Herald, and I naturally was interested, as I thought it was a news item, and I walked across the street. When I got within six feet of the sidewalk, near the drug store, on the corner of 37th Street and 7th Avenue, a policeman stopped me, and asked me, "Where in hell do you live?" I told him in 33rd Street, and then he said, "G— d— you, go home!" and he hit me with his club on the left arm. There were about a dozen policemen standing around there, and two or three within reach. One of these struck me across the right shoulder, and when I turned to run the same policeman, I think, who struck me on the left arm again struck me across the small of my back with his club. Then I limped from there towards the saloon on the southwest corner of 37th Street and 7th Avenue, where a policeman was leaning against a lamppost. As I limped past him he struck me with his club on the right arm. I was then unable to get away from him on account of my injury, but I managed to get across the street and stood in front of the saloon on the southeast corner, and a man came out and asked me to go in. I went in and leaned against a barrel, and he told the bartender that the police had just beaten me. As soon as I was able to walk I started for the New York Herald office to tell the man whom I am employed under. I sat in the chair at the Herald office all night, because there was a great crowd around the street and I was afraid to go home. I left there the next morning about six o'clock, went to my room and changed my clothing, and started for my breakfast. Then I went to the office and worked all day, until about six o'clock that evening. Then I went to my room, and was so lame I could not get out again until the following Tuesday morning, five days after, not even being able, in the meantime, to sit in a chair. I still feel the effects of the clubbing. The blow on the small of my back made my left limb almost paralyzed.

NICHOLAS J. SHERMAN.

Sworn to before me this 24th day of August, 1900.

HERBERT PARSONS, Notary Public, N. Y. County.

Mr. Sherman states in addition that his chief in the newspaper office directed him to report the matter to the police authorities, and that he spoke to Chief Devery, who said to him substantially, "A negro killed a policeman up there, and they can't be controlled."

City and County of New York, ss.:

My name is W. H. Cooper. I reside at 340 West 41st Street. On the morning of August 15th, about half past nine, I went from the house to the post office station at the southwest corner of 41st Street and 8th Avenue. When I reached that corner I saw a group of white men and boys standing at the corner. When I passed this group at this corner I overheard one of them saying, "We are going to get back at the niggers to-night." One of the others said, "Is that true? Is there going to be a riot to-night?" and the reply was "Yes." When I heard this I went around the corner. There was a bicycle pump there. I went behind the bicycle pump like I was looking in the window. I could overhear everything that was said. One of the fellows said, "Have they buried Thorpe, yet?" "No, we expect to bury Thorpe to-day;" and he says, "We expect to have a hot time to-day when the funeral starts." It was rumored around that he was to be buried on the day of the riot, but he was not buried, however, until the next day. One of the fellows said, "Have they got the nigger Harris, yet?" "Yes," he said, "they caught him down at Washington, and if we can get our hands on him we will tar and feather the bastard;" and I went into the drug store and came out again after mailing my letter. When I came out I stood on the corner and filled my pipe, and I overheard them say, "Have they got the woman yet?" and they said, "Yes, she is locked up;" and the other fellow said, "Well, that is all to-night." I did not move on until one of the fellows said, "There is a coon standing there now; you had better hush." Then I went down home and told the boys at the shop about it.

W. H. COOPER.

Sworn to before me this 22nd day of August, 1900.

JOHN C. BARR, Notary Public, Kings County. Certificate filed in N. Y. County.

The Citizens' Protective League was organized in St. Mark's Church, West 53d Street and Eighth Avenue, on Monday morning, September 3, 1900. The object of the League is, first, to afford mutual protection; and, secondly, to prosecute the guilty. The League now numbers about 5,000, with daily increase.

The following officers were elected:

OFFICERS.

Rev. W. H. BROOKS, D.D.,	President.
T. S. P. MILLER, M.D.,	Vice President.
Rev. H. P. MILLER,	Secretary.
JAMES E. GARNER,	Treasurer.

EXECUTIVE COMMITTEE.

T. T. FORTUNE, Chairman,   L. H. LATIMER,

W. R. DAVIS, Secretary,   Rev. R. D. WYN,

C. A. DORSEY,   J. F. THOMAS,

Rev. P. B. TOMPKINS,   N. B. DODSON,

Rev. J. W. SCOTT,   Rev. G. HUNT,

D. M. WEBSTER,   Rev. L. L. CUYLER,

Rev. C. T. WALKER, D.D.,   Rev. H. C. BISHOP,

Rev. W. L. HUBBARD,   Rev. W. D. COOK, D.D.,

Rev. GEO. W. BAILEY,   MELVIN J. CHISUM.

Milton Keynes UK
Ingram Content Group UK Ltd.
UKHW030913151124
451262UK00006B/787